Dear Lizzie

Dear Lizzie

A KIWI SOLDIER WRITES FROM THE BATTLEFIELDS OF WORLD WAR ONE

Edited by Chrissie Ward

HarperCollins*Publishers* New Zealand

To Enid

First published 2000
HarperCollins*Publishers (New Zealand) Limited*
P.O. Box 1, Auckland

ISBN 1 86950 340 6

Designed by Dexter Fry
Typeset by Chris O'Brien
Printed in China

Acknowledgements

My thanks go to David Robinson (Ira's son) for preserving the letters and providing most of the photographs; Janet Braggins, née Brockie (Ada's granddaughter) and Bruce Robinson (Roly's grandson) for their help with family background; and Murray Thacker, Director of the Maori & Colonial Museum, Okains Bay.

Introduction

Ira George Harold Gustavus Robinson was twenty-eight when he joined the New Zealand Rifle Brigade and served with them on the Western Front in the First World War. These letters, written home to his family, provide a fascinating record of his experiences.

Born on 25 August 1888 in Lyttelton, Ira was the youngest of seven surviving children. In 1866 his grandfather, John Robinson, had emigrated from Northern Ireland to New Zealand, where the family settled in various parts of Canterbury, especially Banks Peninsula. Some background information about the Robinsons is given in the appendix on page 138.

Ira's father, William, ran the Okains Bay General Store, a family business which was owned by William's older brother, another John. Ira attended the Okains Bay Primary School from 1893 until 1902, when he passed sixth standard. He must have shown promise, for he was offered a bursary to Christ's College, but he was unable to take it up because the family could not afford the cost of the uniform. Instead he went to Canterbury College of Art, but left after only one year, possibly because of a disagreement with a tutor. He retained an interest in art, and his talent for drawing can be seen in the sketches which illustrate some of these letters.

In 1904 he was apprenticed to a Lyttelton boat builder, one of whose contracts was working on various ships involved in Antarctic exploration at the time. Ira stored some of the wood stripped from Robert Falcon Scott's ship *Discovery*, and after his return from war service he used this to make walking sticks for family members. He also worked for the Railways Department, completing a course which

William Robinson   m. 18 July
b. 25 August 1845
Belfast, Northern Ireland
d. late 1930s

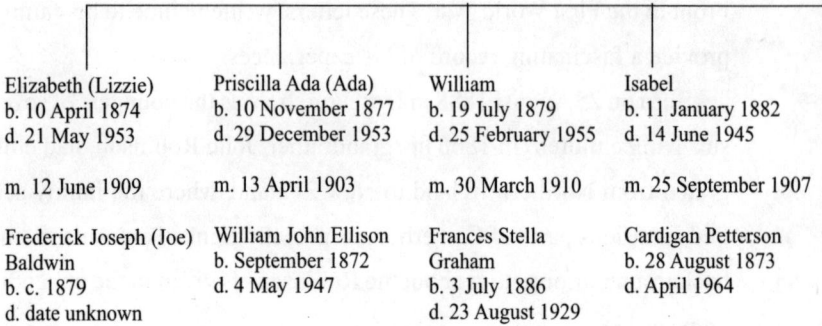

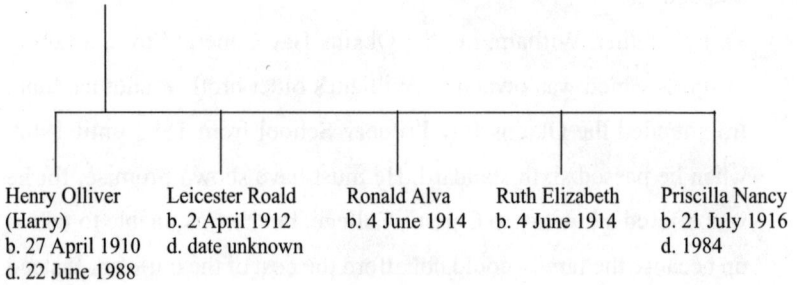

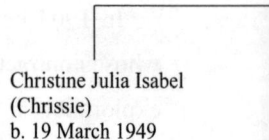

Elizabeth (Lizzie)	Priscilla Ada (Ada)	William	Isabel
b. 10 April 1874	b. 10 November 1877	b. 19 July 1879	b. 11 January 1882
d. 21 May 1953	d. 29 December 1953	d. 25 February 1955	d. 14 June 1945
m. 12 June 1909	m. 13 April 1903	m. 30 March 1910	m. 25 September 1907
Frederick Joseph (Joe)	William John Ellison	Frances Stella	Cardigan Petterson
Baldwin	b. September 1872	Graham	b. 28 August 1873
b. c. 1879	d. 4 May 1947	b. 3 July 1886	d. April 1964
d. date unknown		d. 23 August 1929	

Henry Olliver	Leicester Roald	Ronald Alva	Ruth Elizabeth	Priscilla Nancy
(Harry)	b. 2 April 1912	b. 4 June 1914	b. 4 June 1914	b. 21 July 1916
b. 27 April 1910	d. date unknown			d. 1984
d. 22 June 1988				

Christine Julia Isabel
(Chrissie)
b. 19 March 1949

1873   Priscilla Mary Milsom
b. 16 April 1846
London, England
d. c. 1916

Millicent Olive	Percy Roland (Roly)	Robert (Bob)	Ira George Harold
b. 28 December 1883	b. 3 June 1885	b. 22 November	Gustavus
d. in infancy	d. 7 December 1972	1886	b. 25 August 1888
		d. date unknown	d. 11 April 1959
	m. (1) 4 April 1912		
	Dulcie Muirson		m. 10 August 1921
	b. 27 January 1888		
	d. 15 November 1929		Sarah Isabella (Bella)
			Gibson
	m. (2) date unknown		b. 18 January 1886
	Alice Shaw		d. 13 July 1960
	m. (3) c. 1954		
	Agnes Moorehead		

Enid Mary	David William	Shirley Joan
b. 26 August 1922	b. 17 November 1923	b. 28 April 1925
d. 18 August 1998		d. 31 July 1981
	m. 7 December 1946	
m. (1) 20 February 1947		m. 11 June 1954
	Alison Eva Quickfall	
Travers Burnell Christopher	b. 1 December 1924	Mark Louis
Christie		Johnstone
b. 6 December 1909		b. 19 May 1931
d. 4 January 1974		

m (2) 23 August 1986

John Morrison Carmody
b. 19 November 1923

specialised in locomotive construction. The dates of this are uncertain, but it probably began pre-war and continued for a short time afterwards.

Ira's military service began with his training in New Zealand at Featherston, Tauherenikau and Trentham Military Camps from 2 October 1916 until 13 March 1917. This was probably the first time he had been out of Canterbury. On 14 March he sailed to England, arriving at Plymouth in May. Further training at Sling and Tidworth Camps followed, before the brigade was sent to France in September. He came unscathed through the 3rd Battle of Ypres in October 1917, but was wounded in the thigh on 30 October a year later. The last letter in this collection was written in December 1918 from an English convalescent hospital. He was repatriated to New Zealand on 28 March 1919.

The Robinsons were a close and affectionate family, and much of Ira's free time was spent in writing to them, as well as to the friends and neighbours who wrote and sent the much-appreciated food parcels. The family tree shows Ira's immediate relatives, but his siblings and their spouses need to be briefly described here.

The oldest child was Elizabeth, known as Lizzie (b. 1874), with whom Ira had a particularly close bond. Being fourteen years older, she had probably played an important part in his upbringing. At the age of 35 (unusually late for the period) she married Frederick Joseph Baldwin, known as Joe, who was five years younger than her. Their marriage certificate gives Lizzie's occupation as domestic and Joe's as carpenter, but by the time of the war he had switched to farming.

The next child was Priscilla Ada, known as Ada (b. 1877). She married her first cousin William John Ellison, a saddler.

The oldest son was William (b. 1879). In 1910 he married Stella, the sister of Lewis Graham of Okains Bay, and the couple took over the running of the Okains Bay Store. William was called up in August 1918, but he was still in training in New Zealand when the war ended.

Next was Isabel (b. 1882), who was married to blacksmith Cardigan Petterson.

Then came Percy Roland, known as Roly (b. 1885). His first wife, Dulcie Muirson, was born in Victoria, Australia and came to New Zealand in 1902.

The second to last child was Robert, known as Bob (b. 1886), who never married. Bob was called up in January 1918 and served in France at the same time as Ira, but although the brothers corresponded, they don't appear to have made physical contact there.

The first and fourth of the letters in this book are addressed to Ira's father and the fifth to 'Everybody', but the other twenty-four were written to Lizzie. It was she who preserved them all, she who noted the dates when they arrived and she who wrote on one the instruction, 'Please take care of this letter & return to me.'

Ira was a remarkably prolific correspondent considering the difficulties under which he wrote, whether it was the noise of his fellow soldiers ('I cannot write with all hands talking'), the attentions of lice ('I have to leave off every now and again and snaffle a few of the most bloodthirsty'), or physical discomfort ('I have to lie on my stomach on my bed and write on my pillow, a sandbag full of straw').

This collection contains only a fraction of the letters he wrote home. Many probably never reached their destination, and not all their recipients would have saved them as carefully as Lizzie did. Nevertheless, they span two full years, taking us through Ira's training, his transport to Britain, his impressions of England, both in camp and on leave, and his experiences in France. The optimistic tone of the early letters contrasts with the stark report of his first battle experience in October 1917, which makes, as he says, 'pretty sordid reading'. After this he tries to avoid mentioning the war (although the subject keeps creeping in), and fills his letters with detailed accounts of his daily life and of the people and places he encountered. He had an extremely observant eye and lively powers of description, although his vocabulary was limited by his education. His opinions on 'overseas', sometimes critical and sometimes enthusiastic, provide an insight into life in rural New Zealand at the time. His patriotism and his strongly expressed prejudices, which would raise eyebrows today, were typical of the period.

Awareness of censorship restricted what he could say, but the letters do not, in fact, appear to have been censored at all. However, some of them are so long (up to twenty-two handwritten pages) that it is possible a weary officer would have given them only a cursory reading.

In editing the letters I have corrected the erratic spelling and capitalisation and inserted enough punctuation to clarify meaning, but have avoided any rewriting in order to keep Ira's distinctive voice. That voice brings an individual personality to life, and also speaks as a representative for all the ordinary New Zealand soldiers who served in the 'Great War'.

Chrissie Ward
Nelson

Dear Dad,

I suppose you will be surprised to get a letter from me as I have not written to you at all so far, but I suppose you have seen some of my letters as I have told whoever I have written to, to send the letter on. I cannot write to you all as I do not have the time to do so, so when you have read this letter just hand it on to some of the others.

We were inoculated again last week; this is the second time since we came in to camp. It is supposed to make anyone practically proof against typhoid fever, so if it does that it is worthwhile having a stiff shoulder for a couple of days, which is the only effect it had on me, and also a slight headache – and as we had a whole day off drill we did not mind it so much. Up to the present war, typhoid was the cause of more than half the deaths in the army, and this inoculation has reduced the percentage to about three per cent, so it is evidently some good.

We were shifted back to Featherston Camp last Saturday week from Tauherenikau and I was very pleased, I can assure you, as I did not like the place at all. However, we are here now and having a real good time of it, even if we are drilling a bit harder than previously. We are now getting into the advanced stages of our training, such as bayonet fighting, outpost & scouting work and entrenching, also night marches etc, so you see we are getting on. It is all very interesting and when one goes through it all one begins to realise to what a fine pitch the art of fighting has come. The different stages of the attack under artillery fire are very complicated to explain on paper, but if I come down again I will show you just how it is all done and explain it all to you. That reminds me, I have no idea whether we will get any more leave or not, but I think we will somehow. I hope so, anyway.

We got issued to us what is generally known as the Webb equipment a day or so ago. This is the equipment usually worn by the men in the British Army on active service and I will try and describe it to you, but it will be rather awkward. I'll try, anyway. First of all it is made of a sort of grey-green stiff webbing like very coarse canvas. There is to begin with a broad belt which goes round the waist and is really the main part of the lot, it is about three inches wide and can be shortened or lengthened like an ordinary belt. Then there are two straps which cross on the back, worn one over each shoulder and fastened both back and front to the belt; these are about an inch and a half wide. Now, to the straps which cross on the back is fastened a square bag about 15 inches deep, 12 inches wide across the back and six inches wide from the back to the outside, so:

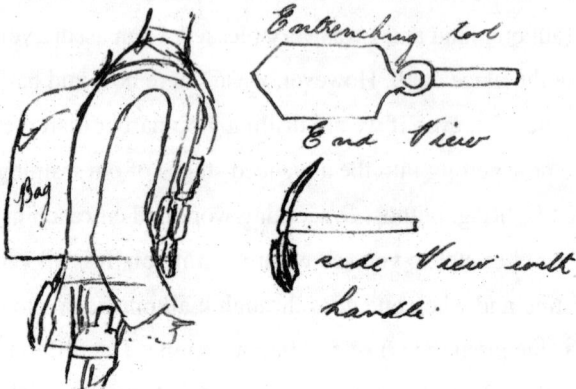

In the bag is carried the greatcoat, mess tin, towel & soap, shaving gear, pair of socks, needle & cotton and any other odds & ends one may need. Now below that we carry the entrenching tool – head shown above. This is used to dig yourself in under fire when you cannot advance any further or are waiting to be reinforced. On the right side, hanging to the belt, is the water bottle, which holds about two pints when full, but we never carry it full while training as drinking on the march is discouraged as much as possible. I nearly forgot, on the straps which come over the shoulders from the back are eight pockets, each of which will hold fifteen cartridges, and the weight of this balances the bag on the back. We carry altogether about 120 rounds of ammunition. We only carry the cartridges when we get into the fight proper, not while training, and we find the equipment heavy enough without them.

Well, to get on. On the left side we carry the bayonet, one of the most important pieces of the turn out, also the handle of the entrenching tool so

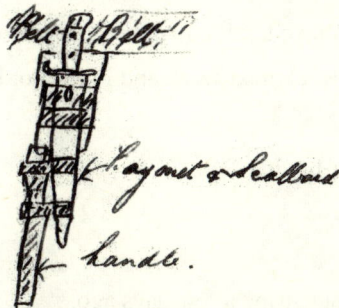

hanging from the belt; on the right side also is carried another smaller bag, about ten by twelve by three, for putting your food and any extra ammunition in when you are going to attack a position.

Besides the gear we have, of course, always our rifle, the most important of all our equipment. So you see we are well loaded up, aren't we, considering we do most of our drill at the double with this rigout on, that is we run nearly all the time. There is one thing that helps us a good deal and that is we wear very little clothes, only a shirt, a short pair of pants, puttees and boots. The short pants, shorts they are called, are just all right as they keep your legs nice and cool. I am sending you a few photos, taken before we had our equipment one day we were on a route march, and that will give you a good idea of what our dress is like when on the march. You will have a job to pick me in the photo as it is not very good as I have shifted, but never mind. I will send some better ones later on.

Well, Dad, I will have to stop now as I want to go to the Army tonight as the South Island has challenged the North Island boys to beat them singing Salvation Army hymns. I would not like to miss it for anything as the singing is very good indeed as a rule – in fact, the best I have ever heard in a church or anywhere else. I can tell you, when 500 of us get going we can sing some. Goodbye for the present, Dad, and love to all down there. Send this letter on as we will have a busy week next week and I may not be able to write again.

I remain, Your Loving Son,

Ira

P.S. Got another stripe a few days ago.

Featherston Military Camp
6 FEBRUARY 1917

Dear Lizzie,

Just a line or so to thank you for the box, or I should say tin, of cakes which you so kindly sent to me. Needless to say they were highly appreciated as they are a vast change from the neverending stew. The stew is all right and all that, but when you get it every day for months on end you get sort of tired of it, I can assure you.

First of all, I hope you and the children are all well again by now as it is just about time you had a bit of change for the better. I got one set of badges for you, the 24th (it is a bulldog), and when I get a few more I will send them to you.[1] It is no use sending one at a time, and the 25th and 26th will be out in a day or so; I will wait till then. I got a parcel of fruit from Dulcie the same day as I got the cakes from you and it seemed quite like Christmas time again. The 22nd RFB, who were to go away last week, were for some reason sent back to Featherston Camp; I don't know why I am sure.[2] As a rule people outside the camp know more of the affairs of the camp than we do inside, as the powers that be don't let us know any more than they can help. Before I go any further, I would like to thank you for the watch which you all gave me. It is a beauty, keeps splendid time, and it is now like a part of my arm as it is always there night and day. I have a ring of white skin round my wrist where it goes and the rest of my arm is as brown as a berry.

We had a Military Sports meeting at Tauherenikau Race Course last Wednesday and my drill squad, at least our squad representing H. Company, won both events which it entered, namely Squad Drill

17

and Rifle Exercises. We, the men, each get £1 out of it, 10/- for each event, and our O.C. shouted us afternoon tea, so we had a good day out altogether.[3] We had another squad in for Bayonet Drill and Physical Exercises – they got one first as well but did not win the other event. Our company won three out of four military events so we did very well, didn't we? On the next day, Thursday, there was a very big Military Sports at Masterton, or at least at Solway, about one mile from Masterton where the Masterton Race Course is, and we entered one squad, the Rifle Exercise & Squad Drill one, and we got two firsts again so we are beginning to kid ourselves somewhat. In fact, we seemed to be in luck all that week as we got the cup which is given to the company which has the best kept lines for the week as well, so we won all along the line. I hope we are as lucky when we get to the front.

I can tell you it is no easy matter to write letters in camp as there is really not much happening that an outsider would understand unless you were to write nearly half a book of explanations, and that would never do. However, our training is getting on all serene and we are more like pack horses now than men, as we wear the Webb equipment all the time at drill now. In my last letter which I wrote to Dad I described it as best I could, so if you get hold of that you will understand pretty well what we are to carry when we are drilling. Some of the boys get air pillows and blow them up and put them in their pack instead of the greatcoat, but that does not always pay as when it comes on to rain an air pillow does not keep the rain off too good. And they also get C.B. 'Confined to Barracks' for doing it as well, that is no leave at all for a certain time.

Talking about air pillows, that one Mary Olliver gave me is just all right and I would not part with it for anything.[4] Tell her so if you see her and tell her I will write some day when I get a chance. She also sent me a lovely cake. In fact, people are so good to me I am spending all my spare time writing and thanking them and now I am sure I have missed some of them, but if they knew the difficulties under which a chap writes here at times they would forgive me, I am sure. Tonight, for instance, there are about six waiting to hop into my chair as soon as I am finished, and I myself am writing against time as there is bathing parade in a few minutes and I have to attend, so I will not be able to write much longer. I have ordered several photos of the H. Co. Squad and I will send you one later on when I get them, but I think they will be in the *Weekly* or *Times* next week anyway so look out for it.

Well Lizzie, I will have to stop now as I must go on parade or get C.B., so goodbye and when I write next I will write a decent letter. So goodbye, with best love to yourself and all the children and all the rest down in ChCh.

I remain, Your Loving Brother,

Ira

P.S. Hope you can read it, have no time to read it through again.
Corporal Robinson IGHG
40846, H Company, 23rds, Featherston

Y·M·C·A
THE NEW ZEALAND EXPEDITIONARY FORCES

WRITE HOME FIRST.

Featherston   **MILITARY CAMP.**

DATE, *Sunday 28 Jan* 1916

~~First~~ of all it is made of a sort of Grey Green stiff webb‸
~~very~~ coarse canvas. There is to begin with a broad
~~which~~ goes round the waist and is really the main
~~the~~ lot, it is about ‸ ‸an be short
~~r~~ lengthens

On Active Service

WITH THE BRITISH EXPEDITIONARY FORCE

~~are~~ exceptionally strong & deep trenches and as
~~Germans held~~ them for nearly two years you
~~may~~ guess that nothing was left undone to help
~~make~~ them as secure from attack as possible.
The forest is on a rise and these trenches are on the
outskirts of it and the sloping grounds which lies
between them and our old Front line which is
about 700 yds away there is just one tangled
mass of rusty barbed wire, stakes both wooden
and iron and pointed on top to make them
more of a nuisance, and all manner of tangled
and twisted angle iron rails iron etc which
~~...~~ed to blow up before they could
~~...~~ now it is smashed up it ~~...~~ to the

~~...~~ that they can tip th‸
~~...~~ way when going unde‸
~~...~~ which are not very
~~...~~ this (in normal position)

~~...~~ two locks on
~~...~~ we were raise‸
~~...~~ next about 6
~~...~~ principle on wi‸
~~...~~ I will not
~~...~~ Joe ought
~~...~~ the beaut‸
~~...~~ the N‸

Ruapehu Troop Ship 79
21 MARCH 1917

Dear Lizzie,

I have been seasick for the last week but tonight I am feeling just all right so I just went and had a piece of that cake I brought from ChCh which you made for me, and as I am doing nothing tonight I thought it would be a good chance to write a few lines to you and then I will be able to send my letter to you at the first opportunity. There is really not much to write to you about as we are not allowed to say anything about our whereabouts etc etc, and anyway, we do not know ourselves as there are not many signposts at sea. However, we are all well and always looking for meal times, which is a good sign.

In the finish we were bustled off in a hurry and I was not able to get some of those badges I was going to for you as they are not making them now, but since I came on board I have found out where I can get several kinds and I will get them later on. I made a bargain with the chap, I am to send him Imperial Badges and he will send some others on to you later on. I am going to send you the two off my collar to make brooches for the girls as soon as we reach our destination.

Hoping you are all well at home as this letter leaves us all on board at present.

I remain, Your Loving Brother,

Ira

P.S. We have to cut our letters short now as the censor reads them all.

P.P.S. As I will very likely lose my stripes on arrival at our destination you had better address my letters Private. If I still have them I will let you know later on.

40846, Private I.G.H.G. Robinson

H Company, 23 Rfts,[5]

G.P.O. Wellington

At Sea
APRIL 1917

Dear Dad,

Just a wee note to let you know we are all getting along fine and
are now having real nice weather, much better than a day or so ago
when it was fairly rough. We have a real good time on board, plenty
of good food to eat, good beds to sleep on, or at least bunks, and just
enough exercise during the day to keep us fit and sleep well at night,
so what more could one wish for? The only thing is that the sea does
not keep smooth all the time, which is rather upsetting I can assure
you. I know all about it, I was bad for about the first week.

We have a band on board, also three pianos, five gramophones,
bagpipes, mouth organs by the dozens, tin whistles and plenty of
good singers, so we have plenty of music. In fact, it is hard
sometimes to get a little quietness to write letters etc, but I am used
to it now and can write through it all. There are about 200 talking
and playing all sorts of games round me now. We also get plenty of
reading matter on board, as many magazines as we can read, and we
also have a real good library with hundreds of first class books in it.
Then we have also all sorts of games and sports such as boxing,
quoits, skipping, touch ball, tug of wars and dozens of indoor
games, so if we do not have a good time it is our fault, don't you
think so? We do not know where we are going or anything about it
so I cannot tell you even if I was allowed, which I am not, and I
expect you will know anyway as soon as we touch anywhere, sooner
than I could let you know.

I will stop now as I have a lot of letters to write yet and I want to make the best of the smooth seas tonight, so I will say goodbye, hoping you are in the best of health and spirits as this letter leaves us all.

I am, Your Loving Son,

Ira

P.S. I am sending you some photos of the 23rds coming over the Rimutakas. I only have one. I want you to keep it for me. Ira.

Sling Camp[6], Salisbury Plain
26 MAY 1917

Dear Everybody,

We arrived in Plymouth, England, last Sunday at about four
o'clock in the afternoon and came to anchor out in the stream
among hundreds of other steamers of all sizes and shapes, but the
Uripides, the boat that came from Cape Town with us, was the
biggest of them all as far as I could judge. They were very careful in
guarding us from submarines during the last few days of the voyage,
and three days or so before we reached port we were met by four
destroyers from Plymouth. The destroyers kept two on each side of
us, and the cruiser which had been with us ever since we left Sierra
Leone kept steaming at full speed round and round the whole lot of
us all the time. She was one of the latest war ships and could steam
about 37 knots an hour and it was a treat to see her going at top.

When we were a day out we were met by two French airships,
which are very wonderful things indeed. They seem to be able to do
just what they like with them and can turn and twist about at any
angle it seemed to me. If the Zeps are better they are hot stuff.[7]
These machines only carry two or three men, so the Zeps must be
very much larger; but all the same these ones are all right anyway.
One of the airships stayed with us until we reached port, the other
one went away out to sea to meet some other steamers coming in.
They say a submarine can be seen quite easily from an airship, no
matter how far they are down from the surface of the water.
However, we never saw any subs and reached port safely, thanks to
the navy. It is a pity our army was not as good and then the Germans

would not have tackled us at all. However, we are learning as we go on and can now more than hold our own, except in a few directions.

Plymouth is a great naval base and the harbour is just crowded with war vessels of all descriptions, from the dingy minesweeper, which is one of the most important branches of the navy now, to the mighty dreadnaught. There are hundreds of destroyers cutting round at top all the time. I forgot to mention – all round outside Plymouth the sea was swept clear of mines by hundreds of minesweepers. On the way in we passed quite close to the Eddystone Lighthouse which is about $7^1/_2$ miles from Plymouth. Our boat, the *Ruapehu*, did not go alongside the wharf; we were taken to the wharf in a ferryboat, which was nearly as wide as it was long and took about six hundred of us at a time. We were landed at the London and South Western Railway wharf and marched straight on board the train and had absolutely no chance to see anything of the town of Plymouth. All I could see was that the houses were as close together as it was possible to put them. There were some very fine buildings facing the waterfront, but I do not know what they were. The railway carriages here are quite different from in NZ. They are partitioned off and each compartment seats about ten, five sitting with their faces to the engine and five facing the opposite way; the doors are locked when leaving the station on both sides and are not allowed to be opened while on the road. We were in third class carriages, the second and first are much wider and have a 'passage' all down one side and are beautifully finished off and upholstered in velvet pile.

This is Saturday night, and as it is nearly time for Lights Out to go and I have not made my bed yet I will have to stop until tomorrow when I may have a little more time to spare. I have not had time to go outside the camp yet, we have been very busy getting settled down.

8.20 SUNDAY MORNING, 27 MAY

We have just finished scrubbing the hut out and cleaning the windows and shelves down and now we are going to get ready for church. It seems rather a farce, to me anyway, but it is the way in the army.

After we were all settled down on the train the engine gave a bit of a whistle and away we went. We travelled for about a couple of miles through the town of Plymouth, and I should say it was the poorer part as the houses looked very dingy and crammed close together and all the same, miles and miles of them. I think they must be the tenement houses we read about, as they are about four storeys high and hundreds of women and children live in them. How they manage it I don't know. It would not suit a N. Zealander very well. However, we soon got out of the town into the country and it was the most beautiful country I have ever seen. The paddocks are as smooth as a lawn and look lovely, especially now the spring flowers are out in bloom. Some of the flowers I do not know the names of, but I recognise a good many of them, one of which is the primrose, which grows wild everywhere, and there are lots of others too, all over the place. The hedges are made of a sod wall with hawthorn or gorse planted on top and they are kept beautifully clipped. What struck me was that the paddocks are all very small and the fences or hedges are very crooked; but there is a reason for both. The reason the paddocks are small is because the farms are small and are cut into small blocks so that the farmer can rest one part and crop another in turn and keep cows etc at the same time, as the farming is very mixed here – cows, sheep, pigs, fowls, crops etc, all on a few acres. The reason the fences are crooked is because the stock need the shelter which they supply during the winter when it is very cold, often two feet of snow, and you can easily understand a crooked hedge makes far better shelter than a straight one does. Another thing I noticed was the way they cultivate the ground. Not one inch is lost as they plough right out to the very edge of the hedges, how they do it beats me. The country is all the same for hundreds of miles on end, just like one big garden all the way.

When we reached a town called Exeter we were given a cup of tea without any sugar in it, as sugar is very scarce in England now, and a small bun, also a card from the Mayoress wishing us good luck etc. I heard one lady say on the station that she had not had any sugar nor a potato for the last six weeks, so you can guess things are not too good here. Church Parade on now.

Have just got back from Church Parade. We were holding it in the open air and a rain storm came on and wet us all through before we could get to the huts again, even at the double; but I must get on with my letter.

We left Exeter at about 3pm as far as I remember now and arrived at Sling Camp, Salisbury Plains at about 5 o'clock. We were detrained and marched straight into camp, with the camp band in the lead. When we got into camp all the NCOs were called out and lined up; then all the men were lined up too, then so many men were cut off and became a Company and the two NCOs, one Sergt and a Cpl, were cut off and put with them. I am in B Company 5th Reserve Battalion of the New Zealand Rifle Brigade, commonly called the

Dinkums, and I do not know one of the men who were put in our Platoon, or I should say Company. I have lost all the mates I had in H Company and goodness only knows if I will be able to pick them up again later on. I am a Lance Corporal now, as all the NCOs who came from NZ lose at least one of their stripes, but get them back again if they are thought competent.

After we were put into companies we were detailed to our respective huts where our beds were already packed up ready to be made with about six clean blankets each bed, and we handed our own blankets, three of them, in to be washed and disinfected, which they badly needed after the trip on the boat. After we got settled in our huts we were turned out straight away and had a nice hot shower which everyone enjoyed. I forgot to mention that we had tea before we had the shower, and although the food is very plain it is beautifully cooked and everyone seems to enjoy it. The huts here are almost exactly the same as at Trentham and the training so far has been exactly the same, but I believe it is different later on. What I like is the way the food is cooked and served up, it is a treat after the boat and Trentham. The waste in New Zealand would feed all the soldiers in the NZRB who are in camp here at the present time, that is the waste in the Trentham and Featherston Camps. Here they waste nothing. Say if a little stew is left, which is not often, the bones are scraped to one end of the dish, the fat to another and the vegetables put in the middle. The plates are scraped into the mess dish and treated likewise, and then the mess dishes are emptied into other big tins outside branded Fat, Vegetables and Bones. If you waste even a crust of bread you are on the mat straight away, as waste here is an absolute wash out. Even the paper is saved and sent away. The mess arrangements here are the only thing that is better than in NZ, otherwise we beat them everywhere, the huts are better, the sanitary conveniences are better and the camp is laid out better than it is here. The discipline here is far ahead of NZ. It is very severe, but if one just does as he is told as quickly as he can not a word is said to him. It is the shirkers who fall in every time and a jolly good job too.

About three miles from here there is an aviation camp and it is nothing to see dozens of aeroplanes in the air at once and they are at it all night long as well. I have only been here a week but do not take a bit of notice of them now, they are so common, more so than the birds, which are very scarce here. Perhaps the aeroplanes have frightened them away? I cannot say. I think that is all I can find to say about the camp just now. I cannot tell you about the surrounding places of interest as I have not been out of camp yet. I forgot to mention the plains here are all covered with round rings like circus rings with a trench round the outside where the Romans used to hold duels, and nearby there are huge mounds where the dead were buried after the scrap was over. If the number of mounds count for anything, they were some fighters were the Romans. The roads in England are beautiful, just like a footpath only very narrow, about half a chain wide.

As I sit writing now I can hear the guns of the RF Artillery going as they are doing a practice over on the plains.[8] There are Australians also in camp here, but they have a camp of their own and have to keep to it, which rule applies to the N. Zealanders as well. We have our own lines, canteen, store and armourer etc, and can go nowhere else except when on leave after parade hours. There are also a lot of Tommies in camp here, the Royal Field Artillery included. The Australians' uniform looks very smart and showy, but the Australian soldier has a rotten name everywhere he goes and in London and Cape Town it is just the same, caused I guess by a few bad eggs among them. Everywhere they are recognised as first class fighters, but the N. Zealanders are equally as good and have a much better name when on leave; they are better behaved somehow. There are 1700 Australians in camp here now with V.D. so you can guess how they behave, but I must not criticise as our chaps are not much better, some of them. It is awful when one thinks of how badly the men are wanted at the Front.

There was an air raid on the SE of England a few days ago, but they don't take much notice of that here although 40-odd were killed and 170 injured.

Well, I will stop now as I consider I have done very well today, so goodbye for the present. Love to all at home in good little New Zealand and God bless you all.

I remain, Your Loving Brother & Uncle,

Ira

P.S. The 22nd left for France last night. When you write address the same as before, they are readdressed in England. Be careful of No.40846 and Initials, GPO Wellington.

Codford Hospital
23 JUNE 1917

Dear Lizzie,

I thought as I had written so often to Dulcie first, I would write
to you for a change this time. I should have been in France now only
I managed to poison my heel, the result of a blister, while on our
final leave in London. We only had four days and I had to leave a
day before it was up and come straight in here, Codford Hospital, so
you can guess it was pretty painful. I have been in here about eight
days now and am just about right again and expect to get emptied
out any time now, but goodness only knows if I will ever see my
mates again as they all went away to France last week.

We are treated very well in here and have rather a good time, all
things considered, and the Sisters are very kind. We had the
Salvation Army padre through here a couple of days ago and he gave
each of the patients a handkerchief, and you can guess mine came in
handy as usual; and another day a lady came through and gave us a
couple of oranges each, so you see we do all right.

There is really not very much to write about now I have got
started so I think I had better try and describe London a little if I
can, but it is not easy as one does not know where to begin. London
is such a big place. To begin with the railway stations in London are
great and the Waterloo Station, where we arrived from Sling Camp,
covers I suppose anything up to twenty or thirty acres and is covered
entirely with glass. There are dozens of trains coming in and going
out all the time, but in spite of that it is no trouble to find any train
you want as the platforms are all numbered in large white letters

and figures like this with the destination of
train and the No. of platform, and you are
not allowed on the platform unless you
have the right ticket. That does away with a
lot of muddling as all the people on the
different platforms know they are in the right places.

I will have to stop now as there is a great argument on in the
ward and I cannot write with all hands talking, so I will stop for
tonight and finish this letter tomorrow when it may be a little
quieter. I will say good night for tonight and write more tomorrow.

SUNDAY 24 JUNE

Before I go on describing London, perhaps it would interest you
to know something of a few of the patients who are in this ward with
me. There are 31 beds and they are nearly always full, of course. I
only know a little about the cases near me. Two beds on the left there
is a Tommy who enlisted in New Zealand and came over here as a
Colonial and broke his leg playing football. He has been in hospital
a good long while and has learned to do all sorts of needlework and
he does it beautifully, all sorts of designs in coloured silks. Not bad
is it, start off to kill German soldiers and finish up making table-
centres etc. Next to him there is a farmer from the Waikato who is
recovering from pluricy – that doesn't look as if it is spelt right, but
that does not matter. He reads nearly all the time and is very nearly
blind and wears specs, of course. Then comes my bed. On the other
side is an Australian who has done about ten months in France and
then suddenly discovered that his back is bad, and when he was put
under X Rays they find out he has quite a big bent in his spine and

he will have to go away back again. Next to him is a jockey from Riccarton, ChCh. He has a sprained ankle and is a jolly hard case and keeps us all awake when we ought to go to sleep, telling us horrible tales of his training exploits. He is a lovely liar, he is only wasting his time in the army. Next to him is another N.Zer. who is just recovering from pneumonia. Next is another NZ boy with a bad knee and he is a good mate for the jockey; in fact, they are mates and came over together in the 23rds second half. Then comes another Ausy, as they are called all over England. He takes fits and is a wee bit short into the bargain. When he was coming in to camp a girl gave him a bun and a cup of tea on one of the railway stations and he has been writing to her ever since. Next is a chap who was in the artillery in the retreat from Mons. He was in the Imperial Army then and I don't know what he is doing in a NZ ward now, I am sure. A horse fell on him and injured his stomach and he cannot eat anything solid now although he is a fine big man. Then comes a young chap named Conway. He comes from Wainui, you know, near Akaroa, and is just getting over a very severe attack of pneumonia which nearly settled him. He can just manage to hobble with two sticks now.

The rest on this side I don't know much about at all except that they are nearly all N. Zealand boys. On the opposite is a Maori boy with something the matter with his side. Then there are half a dozen who are just about all right and will be tipped out along with me in a day or so. Then comes the most interesting case in the ward. He is a Belgian who was in Antwerp when the Germans started to walk over Belgium. He was in the retreat from Antwerp and was taken prisoner, but he and a dozen others escaped and came across to England, but not before he had been wounded by a bayonet which very nearly settled him. He lost three brothers and four sisters and both his parents. His wife had just gone out to Australia and missed it all as luck would have it. After being wounded he was discharged and joined his wife in Aus. However, he could not settle down and enlisted with the Ausy lot and he came back to England, but the training was too much for him and his old wound broke out again; but he is hopeful and reckons he will get over and have another smack at them.

Next comes a young chap from ChCh called Lander, and he is another character and keeps one laughing all the time. He has been over to France, also in Egypt, and he has seen a good deal of active service and tells some very tall yarns, but it all helps to make a bit of fun. Then comes another Ausy who was over in France for about a week and managed to get a hit in the jaw with a bullet, which is supposed to stop him eating hard food, but he is only swinging the lead and the sinner eats more than any of us and is as fat as a hog, which he is anyway. He is an awful skite and to hear him talk you would think he had put in at least a couple of years at the front. He gets on my nerves. The next is another Ausy who got in the dingbats and fell over some timber and hurt his head, but he is all right again now and what they are keeping him here for now beats me. I think that is about all that would interest you, except that nearly all the Sisters are New Zealand girls and they are just all right and are kindness itself. Just to give you an instance of their kindness, one of the Sisters went out the other night and paid for enough strawberries to go round the whole ward, about 30 of us altogether.

I had better get on with my letter again now, I suppose. When you get off the train at Waterloo Station, as is only natural you feel as if you would never find your way anywhere, there is such a crowd flying about; but strange to say London is easier to get about in than what ChCh is, the motor buses are great. Well, to begin with we took a trip in a tube railway – they are great, I can assure you. You go down in a lift to get to them and trains, stations and everything are under ground, and in spite of all that the air is always beautifully fresh and there is usually a good breeze blowing. They are electric trains and have about two trailers on each of them and travel like fun and are very cheap travelling indeed, and everyone uses them except strangers, who don't for two reasons. The first is that you usually have to change trains once or twice, and unless you understand the system or have a Londoner with you, you are very likely to land up in some place where you had no intention of going at all. The second is that strangers usually want to see as much of London as possible and the top of a bus is just about the best place to do so. The buses run everywhere and the people use them the same as we do the trams in ChCh, the only difference is that they run about every half minute and you can go quite a long way for a halfpenny. Travelling is about the only thing that is cheap in the Old Country. Everything else is very dear indeed, especially food, which is getting scarce, I can assure you. The German blockade is not such a paper blockade as the people in the Colonies are led to believe. I can assure you it is absolutely the worst feature of the whole war. That reminds me, while we were on leave in London there was an air raid and about 50 were killed and nearly 500 injured, so the air raids are not to be sneezed at either.

Well, to get on. There are very few electric trams in London, but they say in the suburbs there are more. The people stick to the bus in London itself. As a town I was terribly disappointed with London.

The shops there are not a patch on ChCh even, except in a very few cases, although they must be very beautiful inside by the descriptions I have heard of some of them, but they make a very poor window display as far as I could see, and most of the shops are only about twenty feet wide as the street frontage is very dear either to buy or rent. Some of them are very quaint old places and would just suit you down to the ground, and goodness only knows when they were built. When I was in London I bought a good many regimental badges and sent them to Dulcie to keep for me, and when I get a chance I will get some more and send them back to NZ. I think I sent about 100 altogether, some of them are real good ones. Get Roly to fetch them out for you to have a look at.

We went, like most New Chums, to see the Tower of London and I could have stayed in there a week, but unfortunately we only had about a couple of hours. We saw the cell where the two little Princes were smothered, also the cell where Guy Fawkes was kept while waiting for trial, and the cell where Walter Raleigh was kept for thirteen years, and the rooms and cells where dozens of notable Queens, Kings and Princes were imprisoned before they were executed or brought up for trial. Some of the carving on the walls of the cells is very beautiful. It was done by the prisoners during their long terms of imprisonment, it must have been awful. It quite gave me the blues, although it was all very interesting.

What I liked the best was the old suits of armour. There are hundreds and hundreds of suits of it, whole rooms full, and truly it is most wonderful, the workmanship is simply marvellous. Just fancy, a whole suit of armour, perhaps a hundred pieces in all, and the whole of it inlaid with brass or copper. It looks beautiful. How in the world it was possible to do it at all beats me, it cannot be done now, and it is made so that the movements of the body and arms are not restricted in any way. Some are made of steel alone and engraved and I never saw anything to equal it, it is wonderful, and some of the breast pieces are reckoned to be the finest pieces of engraving there is in existence. That was the room that I liked the best in the whole Tower. There were also suits of Japanese armour made of leather and they were very wonderful pieces of work too, but I liked the steel ones myself. In the same room is kept poor Earl Kitchener's sword, also the sword which the Japanese people presented to him soon after the war began, you will remember the occasion. It is over 500 years old and they say it has never been cleaned although it is like a piece of brightest silver. It is a very beautiful piece of steel. Poor old Lord Robert's revolver is in the same box as Kitchener's swords, also the famous letter in which K of K appealed to the men of London for another 100,000 men.[9] It was bought for £6,000 and presented to the Tower authorities.

There is another room in the Tower where all the cannon that has been captured for the last 500 years is kept. Of course, it is not all there, but they keep a sample of each. Some of the old pieces which were taken from the Chinese and Burmese hundreds of years ago are really wonderful. The whole cannon is made to represent a dragon and is hand worked from end to end, and the gun carriage as well. How in the world they ever did it beats everyone nowadays. It cannot be done now. We also saw the block and axe that was used to execute all the prisoners in the Tower, and the place in the Tower enclosure called the Tower Green, where the block used to stand. I could write a good deal more about the Tower, but it is rather dismal so I will stop. I might mention that right round the Tower is a huge moat, about three chains wide, which used to be kept full of water in the olden times. What do you think it is used for now? It is dry now and it is where hundreds of the boys are trained for the front, so you see the old Tower has come in handy again after many years. There are also dozens of anti-aircraft guns mounted round the Tower and they did good work during the raid last week. The raid was right over that part of London.

From the Tower we went to St Paul's Cathedral and I don't know I am sure whether I should attempt to describe it or not. Look here, Lizzie, it is simply magnificent and I don't know I am sure which part of it I like the best. I have never seen or dreamed of anything so beautiful as the altar; it is a mass of carved marble and gold, and the font is also beautiful. The bottom of the altar is a picture of the Lord's Supper, not painted, but inlaid in porcelain or some other kind of stuff, and it is a wonderful piece of work. The rest of the altar is composed of carved marble pillars with sprays of golden vines climbing up them and on the top of each pillar a carved figure, but it cannot be described so that you would have any idea of its loveliness. It beats me altogether. Then the carving on all the woodwork is something wonderful, I cannot describe it all to you, it would take me a month; and then the ceilings are all beautifully inlaid with beautiful pictures, and in fact everything from the roof to the floor is one mass of lovely carving or painting. Everything has been made beautiful, no matter how much trouble or money it may have taken. Here we saw the tomb of Nelson and dozens of other notable men in the history of England. They are laid to rest in the vaults under the church, and the monuments and tablets erected to them are very wonderful and beautiful. I noticed one there to the memory of the late Richard Seddon; also one to Sir George Grey. There is in St Paul's what is known as the whispering gallery. It is said that no matter how softly you whisper on one side of the gallery, it can be distinctly heard on the other side. It is away up in the dome and as we never had much time we did not go up there. I was going up next day but I landed up in Codford Hospital instead.

We also saw Westminster Abbey and it was much the same as St Paul's, only it is hundreds of years older. The historical events connected with the Abbey are the most interesting part of it, but all the same some of the work inside is most beautiful. This is where the coronation takes place, but we did not see the Coronation Chair as it has been removed to a safe place while the air raids are on, a wise precaution too, just now. I also went to see the Royal Academy, and you talk about pictures! I never thought it was possible for anyone to paint anything so real. Some of the pictures of little kiddies, you would not be at all surprised to step clean off the canvas, they are that real. The only thing, I was pushed for time there as usual and only had a couple of hours altogether, but if I ever get to London again I will have another look at it. We also went to the waxworks, Madam Tussauds, you know, but I did not enjoy it very much as my heel was very painful that afternoon.

I will stop now Lizzie, as it is tea time and I want to write a few more letters today, but they are not all going to be as long as this one. So goodbye, with love to all in good old NZ.

I remain, Your Loving Brother,

Jra

P.S. Please send letter on when you have done with it.

Sling Camp
9 AUGUST 1917

Dear Lizzie,

I wrote a long letter to Bob a few days ago in answer to one I received from him and I suppose eventually you will receive it to read, but I thought as I had ten minutes to spare before tea tonight (we were marking on the butts today and finished early) I would drop you a few lines. First of all, I am back in Sling Camp. We marched over from Codford on Tuesday last, the 7th, and I was not sorry to get away from Codford as it was a very dull place. I feel quite at home here as I know a lot of the boys in the 24th and 25th who are also in camp here just now. Among them is young Jack Ware, the two Mason boys, who I have not dropped across yet, Roger and Mick, Gray the schoolmaster from Akaroa, and several boys I met up at Oxford and elsewhere.[10]

The weather has been rotten here lately. It has rained a part of nearly every day and the place is in an awful mess with mud, caused by so many men tramping about. However, I am an old hand by now and can manage to keep pretty dry in spite of the wet. It was beautiful this morning but is raining again now, and I am on duty tonight so I hope it clears up soon. I am on a picket to Bulford, which is about a couple of miles from here. We are supposed to keep order there, but it is really a farce as the picket are about the only soldiers one sees in Bulford.

I believe we are to go over to France on Sunday or Monday next, but I am not sure as they tell us absolutely nothing of what they are going to do with us until just before they want it done, and then you

41

have to do it mighty quick.

Well, I will have to stop now as the mob is in for tea, so goodbye with love to all.

I remain, Your Loving Brother,

Jra

Rifle Brigade, Tidworth Camp
19 August 1917

Dear Lizzie,

I received your letter along with sixteen others from various people last Thursday afternoon and I can tell you I had a great time of it reading all of them, especially as I had not received one letter for weeks and weeks. As you see I am still in England and I have no idea when I will be going over to France as I expected to be away weeks ago and I am still here. There is a rumour that we may go over at the end of this week, but I cannot say for certain as we are not told a word until the last minute. We are not in Sling Camp now, as you see. We shifted from there last Thursday and we are now camped here in tents, and I can tell you it is pretty rough as we are not properly settled down yet and the cooks have to cook everything outside over the open fire. As there are 2,500 of us here, all Rifle Brigade men, you can guess they have their work cut out. However, they are experts at their work and all things considered we are fed very well indeed.

Tomorrow, Monday, the whole of the Rifle Brigade is to be inspected by the Duke of Connaught, who is the honorary head bummer of the brigade.[11] It ought to be a good turn out but I am living in hopes that I will not be in it, as you can see more if you are a spectator. Anyway, being in it yourself is no good as you have to stand like a stuffed monkey while a dozen or so of the heads, or tin hats as we call them, glare at you and try and find some fault with the way your boots are laced up or something else equally as trifling; it is enough to make one sick of the army altogether. However, I

43

think I can manage the spectator stunt all right as about forty of us who have finished our training have been doing all the fatigue work about the camps, both here and in Sling, patiently waiting for orders to go overseas. The 26th and 27th Rfts, or part of them, have arrived safely in England about last Wednesday, and on Thursday some went into Sling Camp and some came on to our camp at Tidworth to make up Rfts for the Rifle Brigade. The poor chaps who came here had rather a bad time of it. They did not get here until midnight, and as they had a couple of cases of smallpox on board the boat on the way over they were isolated from us and for the first night slept without any blankets even, only just their overcoats. I guess they will not forget the first night they spent in Old England in a hurry. All they got to eat was a few biscuits and a drink of tea without much sugar in it and well smoked into the bargain. However, they are all right now and are out of isolation and are beginning to find some of their old mates over here in the 24th and 25th Rfts.

Talking about meeting boys you know over here, Jack Ware and the two Mason boys, Mick and Roger, are all here in the 24th. As I sit writing now I can look out of my tent door and see Jack Ware cleaning his boots and brass ready for the review tomorrow, and it puts me in mind of the old jolly times we had in Okains Bay. It seems like half a century ago, such a lot of things have happened in the meantime. Anyway, we all have the satisfaction of knowing that we were a jolly happy family and had a real good time, and that is something to look back on with pleasure.

This is the greatest place I have struck yet for aeroplanes, and as I write now I can hear half a dozen of them buzzing about overhead like monster bumblebees. They are simply marvellous machines and the airmen can do almost anything in them, even to flying upside down, diving for hundreds of feet towards the earth and then gliding gracefully away to one side and doing all manner of mad antics. Sometimes two battle planes go up and practise fighting one another in the air and I can tell you, until you are used to seeing them at it, the capers they cut make your hair stand on end. Some of the machines can travel at the rate of 200 miles an hour, and the airmen are strapped in them before they leave the ground and if anything goes wrong they have not a ghost of a chance of escaping. Five were killed last week in one flying school alone near Sling Camp. I am sending you a picture of one of them. It is the only one I can find just now, although I had about half a dozen different pictures of different kinds a few days ago before we shifted; but I suppose they are lost, as a lot of stuff usually goes astray when shifting.

I got the piece of maidenhair fern all right and I just fancied I could see Joe's fernery under the tanks at the back of the house. Since I returned to camp from hospital I have had another two days' leave and I spent both of them in London. I managed to find out R. Ellison's address, his business one, by calling at the High Commissioner's Office, and after an hour or so discovered his office in Tooley Street, only to find that he and his family had that morning left for Margate to spend a couple of weeks at the seaside, so I spent the rest of the day wandering about all over London.[12] I tried to get something to send back to you all, but everything is so dreadfully dear now I could not manage it, as I can only draw 1/9 a day over here. If one cables for money it has to come through the defence people and the beggars will not give it to you unless you are going on fourteen days' leave. Red hot, isn't it? I know one chap who has had £10 in London waiting for him for months. The returned boys say France is a much better place to buy anything to send home. Things are not half so dear over there as in London.

I was pleased to hear the children were all doing so well. I will hardly know them when I come back, they will have all grown so much, especially the baby, Nancy – she will be quite grown up by then. I suppose Harry and Lester are growing up too, and evidently are pretty hard cases.[13] They must not expect too much of their Uncle Ira as he is only one in about eight million, but I will do my best and no one can do more. Anyway, I think we have old Fritz on toast and we can give him more than he wants any time, but are playing the waiting game, which does not suit him at all.

However, enough about the war. It is no use talking about it. I was going to tell you, on my second day of leave in London I went for a trip up the river Thames on an excursion steamer which sails from Westminster Bridge at eleven am and gets back at eight pm, which makes a good long day of it. You can enjoy it all the time, it is very interesting all the way, and when you get well up the river it is very beautiful. Down in London the river is full of barges. There are thousands of them, and you will see a fussy little steamer with about a dozen of them in tow and making as much fuss as an ocean liner. What amused me was the fact that their funnels are made with a hinge at the bottom so that they can tip them down out of the way when going under some of the bridges which are not very high. They are made like this:

(in normal position)   [in use]

We went through two locks on the way up. In the first we were raised about 4 feet and in the next about 6 feet, but as you know the principle on which the locks are worked I will not attempt to describe it to you.

Joe ought to have been there to see the beautiful summer residences of the nobs, he would be in his glory. Talk about lawns! That is the place to see them. It is simply lovely. There are no fences or hedges on the river bank and the lawns run right down to the water's edge. There is usually a beautiful old English house covered with ivy at the back, with about an acre or so of lawn in front and perhaps a couple of summerhouses and a rose garden with the roses all out in bloom. Then right on the river bank they cut out an oblong piece, usually on one side of the front of the lawn, and let the water come in. Over this is built a pretty little boathouse, and in nearly all of them are housed the most beautiful motorboats I have ever seen. When they want to go for a run in their boat they simply walk down the lawn to the boathouse, step into the boat, which is usually upholstered in velvet or plush with electric lights etc, and away they go. It must be grand. This place would suit Roly and Joe fine. Roly could drive the motorboat up the river and see all the hundreds of different kinds of motorboats, punts, houseboats and yachts and canoes. I had no idea there were so many different kinds of motorboats in existence. They are all there, from the old barge laden with coal to the very latest racing freak. Then Joe could sit in the stern and see enough different styles and shapes of gardens, summerhouses etc to do him all his life. I only wish they may have the opportunity some day when the war is over. We also saw dozens of houseboats, and they are great. They are quite big affairs, some of them must have about six or eight rooms in them, bathroom, electric light, hot and cold water, and a big deck on top where the people hold dances. This deck is lit at night by Chinese lanterns and must look very beautiful. I did not come back by the boat as I was pressed for time, I had to report at camp that same night. I took a tram which runs from Hampton Court, where the boat stops, to London.

I was pleased to hear that Joe's potatoes, or spuds – a potato by any other name is just as good, you know – have been a success. I am also glad he is getting a good price for them, if things are as dear in NZ as they are over here. On the riverboat it cost me 3/- for a plate of cold ham and salad and 5d extra for a cup of tea and bread and butter, and if you had jam another 3d. So you see you cannot make 1/9 a day go very far, can you, and then there was no sugar in the tea either, which did not suit me at all, I can assure you.

Guess who is in the same tent as me? Jack Hayward, a son of Hayward the painter and paperhanger in Akaroa who papered the passage in our old house in Okains Bay years and years ago. It is strange where one meets people, isn't it?

I will now close, Lizzie, with love and best wishes to you all in Papanui, ChCh and the Bays, where I hope you will send my letter when you have read it. I do not get enough time to write long letters to each one every mail, although I would like to, but I know you will understand that, as a soldier's time is never his own. Even now, 8.30 pm Sunday night, I have to clean my brass and I have been working all day as well, even if it is Sunday. Keep the postcard and I will try and get more later on if I get a chance. Goodbye, with love to all.

I remain, Your Loving Brother & Uncle,

Ira

P.S. The watch is going splendid and has not given one minute's trouble since I left NZ. It is a beauty.

P.P.S. If anyone sends anything let it be solid chocolate, as I am dying for something sweet.

THE NEW ZEALAND EXPEDITIONARY FORCES

WRITE HOME FIRST.

Featherston _____ MILITARY CAMP.

DATE, *Sunday 28 Jan* 1916

First of all it is made of a sort of Grey Green stiff webb

very coarse canvas. There is to begin with a broad

which goes round the waist and is really the main

the lot, it is about ⸺ ⸺ can be short

r lengthen⸺

t⸺

On Active Service

WITH THE BRITISH EXPEDITIONARY FORCE

are exceptionally strong & deep trenches and as

Germans held them for nearly two years you

ay guess that nothing was left undone to help

make them as secure from attack as possible.

The forest is on a rise and these trenches are on the

outskirts of it and the sloping grounds which lies

between them and our old Front line which is

about 700 yds away there is just one tangled

mass of rusty barbed wire, stakes both wooden

and iron and pointed on top to make them

more of a nuisance, and all manner of tangled

a twisted angle iron railway iron etc which

⸺ to blow up before they could ⸺ it as smashed up it

that they can tip th⸺

way when going und⸺

which are not very

this

(in normal position)

h two locks on

we were raise⸺

le next about

principle on wi⸺

I will not

Joe ought

the beau⸺

France

13 S<small>EPTEMBER</small> 1917

Dear Lizzie,

After waiting ever so long I received eleven letters all at once last night, among them being three from you which, needless to say, I was very pleased to receive. I was sorry to hear that the children had not been too good, but I guess by the time you receive this letter the fine weather will be here once again and they will soon shake off their colds.

I have not been in the trenches yet, but it will not be very long before I am there now and if I am lucky I may be back in Blighty with a nice wee smack.[14] At least that is what the old hands say, but all the same I don't want that as I prefer a whole skin as long as possible. Anyway, it is not worth bothering about either way.

What I have seen of France it is much the same as England – but I don't fancy the Froggies at all, what I have seen of them. They are mostly very dirty themselves, and some of the villages we passed through were absolutely filthy and smelt in proportion to the filth. I will not be able to write much today as we are to move tomorrow morning and have a terrible lot to do this afternoon. Medical inspection, kit inspection, C.O. inspection and goodness knows what not; I will be lucky if I am allowed to finish this wee note in peace. Some of the French girls are very pretty and have the most beautiful hair and teeth, also complexions if they would only wash enough of the dirt off for one to see it. Of course, we only saw the peasant class and they are mostly pretty low, at least the ones we see about the boundaries of the camp. When on the march dozens of these girls follow us along the road and sell us apples, pears and chocolate for about three times as much as they are worth. Very good of them, isn't it?

I have written you several letters from England. I hope you will get some of them anyway, and whatever happens I hope you will not think I am not writing whenever I get a chance, which has not been very often lately. As for the badges I sent to the wee girls, I sent a whole lot more from London and I hope they will arrive in NZ safely, as they are a good collection and I would like you to see them all together. When I get back I will have several more I hope to divide amongst you all, and if I don't come back I would like you to all have some each. I heard about Tess Ware from Jack Ware who was in a tent next to mine while in camp in England – strange, wasn't it? – and I see Mick Mason in camp here, also Roger and one of the Mould boys.[15] I don't think you need worry about Joe as the war will either be lost or won before much longer, as neither side can last for ever the way things are going.

I was surprised to hear about Uncle Olliver as he looked so well the last time I saw him. Poor old man, I guess he kept going till the last, which I guess is the best way.

Well Lizzie, I will have to close my letter now as we fall in in a few minutes. So goodbye with love to you all, and tell Harry I will be looking for that handkerchief as the cold weather is coming on now, and I will try and write to him later on.

From your Loving Brother,

Ira

P.S. Hope you can read this as I have not time to correct it.

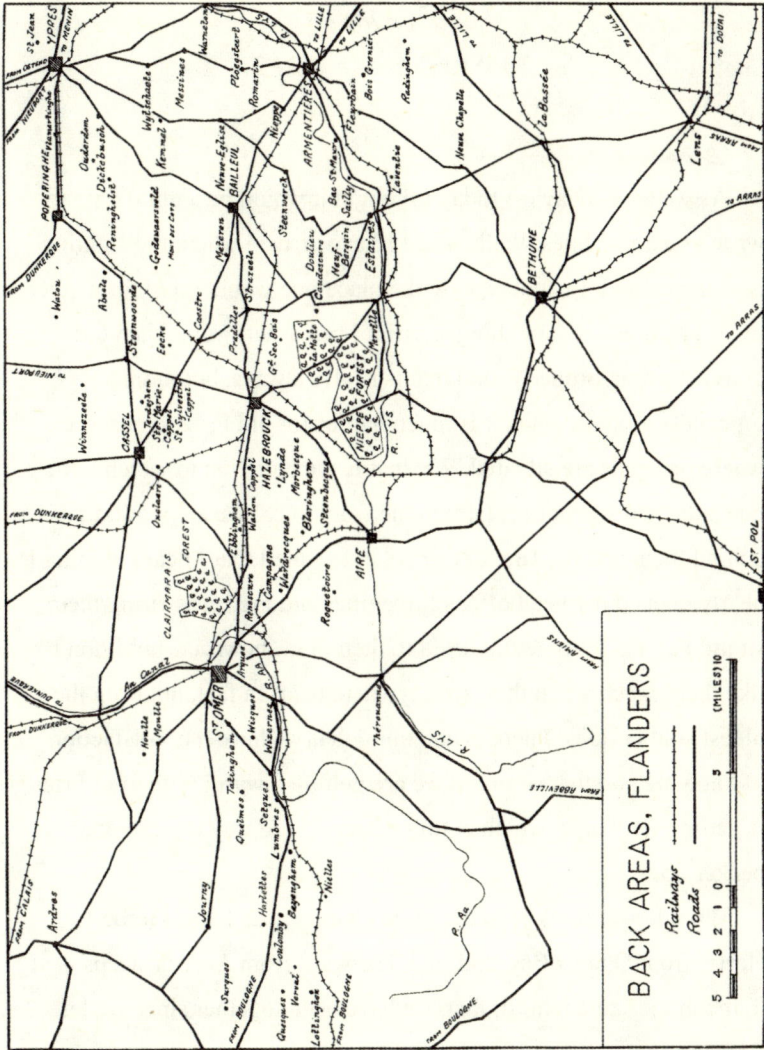

BACK AREAS, FLANDERS

From The History of the Canterbury Regiment N.Z.E.F. 1914–1919, *Captain David Ferguson, M.C., Whitcombe and Tombs, Auckland, 1921.*

France

26 SEPTEMBER 1917

Dear Lizzie,

As we have a day off today I thought it would be a good time to write you a few lines. Well, at last I have arrived where the fighting is going on and it is not exactly the place one would go to for a quiet time. The noise is something terrific, I can assure you, when the guns are going properly; and that is nearly always, but more especially at night when it is much harder for old Fritz to observe where our guns are situated. We, that is the battalion to which I am now attached, are not actually in the front lines. We are working just behind them and the first day or so, every shell that I heard coming I nearly ducked my head off, as I imagined old Fritz was firing them straight at me. I am getting used to them now, however; but I don't like them much when they are anywhere near. In fact, not even the oldest soldier does. There is one thing that we have the satisfaction of knowing and that is, that if we are getting a warm time of it, Fritz is getting far worse, which at times goes a long way to keep one's pecker up.

Who do you think is in the same Company as I am? Herbert Harris from Okains Bay, and Jack Hayward from Akaroa sleeps next to me in the same tent. In fact, we have been together since we left England some time ago.

My word, Lizzie, it is a good job the Germans never got in to England. The way they have smashed the towns in France up is something terrible. From where I am sitting writing now I can see what remains of what was once a good big town with a population of about 20,000.[16] Now there are about a dozen houses, all of which have had to be practically rebuilt, and the shattered walls and part of the steeple of a big church, or cathedral, it is hard to say which it has been. As for the poor people who used to live there, they have gone long ago. The British occupy the town now, but the enemy can still put shells in it with his big guns, which throw a shell between twenty-five and thirty miles. As I said before, if he can shell us, we can shell him, and I can see a couple of big naval guns giving him something to go on with this morning; also I can hear them, as they make an awful roar when they go off. One very strange thing I noticed about the big guns, and that was you can hear the shells tearing through the air fully ten or fifteen seconds after they leave the muzzle of the gun. Before I go any further I will tell you my new address, which we have to put in the middle of our letter. We are not allowed to put it at the end. It is Rifleman I.G.H.G. Robinson 40846, C Company, 12th Platoon, 2nd Battalion, New Zealand Rifle Brigade, France.

There used to be a good many aeroplanes over in England I thought, but this is the place to see them. They fly about here in flocks and I saw over twenty of them in the air at once the other evening. Old Fritz has any amount as well, but his are too far away for us to see, except when he comes over our lines or camps to drop bombs on top of us, when we can see far too much of them. The planes are used mostly as scouts and are the eyes of the artillery and report to the gunners where their shells are landing and whether to lengthen or shorten their range or alter the direction either to the right or left. Also they find out the whereabouts of Fritz's batteries and whether he is moving troops etc, and report to their batteries who give them a lively time, I can assure you.

Well Lizzie, I could write a whole lot more about the war etc, but we are not allowed to say very much, but I think it will be over before New Year. I hope so, anyway. I will stop now as it is dinner time, so goodbye with love to all.

I remain, Your Loving Brother,

Ira

The Robinsons' store at Okains Bay, c. 1890. William Robinson stands directly outside the shop, his wife Priscilla by the open gate, and Lizzie at the far right, wearing a white apron.

The Okains Bay General Store today.

Priscilla Mary Robinson (née Milsom), Ira's mother.

William Robinson, Ira's father.
Cartes de visite,
Canterbury Museum, 16306

The three younger Robinson brothers, c. 1890. Left to right: Bob, Ira, Roly.

The Robinson sisters of Okains Bay, c. 1890. Lizzie seated right, Isabel seated centre, Ada standing. Seated left is Lizzie Rosewarne, a teacher at Okains Bay Primary School, who boarded with the family.

Corporal Ira Robinson of H Company, 23rd Reinforcements, New Zealand Rifle Brigade, while in training at Featherston Military Camp, 1916.

'Nearly forgot. This is H Company's Squad Drill & Rifle Exercise Team which got first in both events at the Tauherenikau Military Sports and two firsts at the Masterton Military Sports held a couple of weeks ago. We kid ourselves a bit although we all look so unhappy. This was taken at the Tauherenikau Sports.' Ira Robinson first left, front row. See letter dated 6 February 1917, page 17.

In Billets, France
21 October 1917

Dear Lizzie,

I think I wrote my last letter to Ada about a couple of weeks ago, but it seems like years to me, such a lot has happened in the meantime. When I wrote last I think I told you not to be surprised if you did not receive letters regularly from then on; my reason was because we were to go over the top a day or so after I had written my letter, and one never knows what may happen. However, we have been over and got a terrible rough handling, which I will describe to you later on in my letter, and I am thankful to say I never got even a scratch. How I escaped I cannot understand, unless it is because I have so many praying for my safe return to New Zealand. My three mates were all wounded, Jack Hayward from Akaroa being among them, and another ChCh boy called Davies, late of Davies & Lamb Hairdresser etc, and another called Stewart from Otago. I am going to describe the attack to you and it will make pretty sordid reading, but it will give you some idea of what we had to go through up there; but it was an exceptionally bad place.[17]

Well, we had bad luck right from the start, and the night before we moved up near the front line one of Fritz's planes dropped bombs on our camp, killing two and wounding five. By the way, Jack Ware was only a few yards away from where the bomb dropped, but he escaped then. I think, but I am not sure, that he was wounded in the advance. He is in the NZRB but is in a different Coy to me. He is in D, I am in C Coy.

We started at about 5pm, just as it was getting dark, and quietly left our camp near Ypres. Each man was well loaded up with rifle, bayonet and ammunition, equipment, steel helmet, two bombs, shovel, six sandbags, one rifle, grenade, oil sheet, overcoat and two days' rations and a full water bottle, also a pair of socks, knife, fork and spoon and two gas helmets, which altogether I can assure you weigh a good deal, about 60 pounds or more. Well, we set out and our troubles began. With this load up we started to walk along about 4 miles of duckboards, as we call them; at least we were on the boards sometimes, at others we were in the mud alongside where we had slipped off into mud up to our knees. It was awful, I can tell you, and old Fritz shelled us all the way and our own guns were blazing away round us also, so you can imagine what the noise was like. At least you cannot imagine, but you can try.

After walking about four hours in the dark and rain – it now started to rain – we were halted and told to make ourselves as comfortable as we could, which meant we were to dig in and try and get a little sleep if we could. Our section, the Bombers, dug in and were not so bad for a while in spite of the wet and old Fritz's shells, which were falling thick and fast all round and among us. Then the water started to come in the trench and a little later the sides of the trench fell in and we had to dig it out again. Altogether we dug it out three times that night, and in between we bailed the water out with a bully beef tin. You can imagine the amount of sleep we got, as it was very cold and rained all the time. However, we got through the night somehow and had to remain in the trench all the next day, showing ourselves as little as possible so that Fritz would not know we were there. We put in the day somehow and remained in the trenches where we were until about 1.15am on Sunday morning, when we moved up just behind our front lines ready to hop over, and again sat in shell holes etc for three or four hours waiting for the word to advance.

Just as the dawn was breaking our barrage opened up and we got the long-looked-for word to advance. We hopped over, that is our platoon, with our officer Mr Vaun in front, and from then on it was just one horrible nightmare.[18] There were the boys getting killed all round us, some of them getting the most terrible wounds. It was awful. Our Company went in with 146 men and came out with 40, the rest were either killed or wounded. However, one has no time to notice much and we advanced in spite of old Fritz and we captured his front line of trenches and several machine guns, also a good many prisoners. All the time our boys were getting fewer and fewer. After we got the first line I never saw my mates again, and only after we came out did I find out they were wounded. We kept on going for about 800 yds, where we were held up by two pillboxes which our artillery had failed to smash. There we had to dig in under old Fritz's rifle and artillery fire, which was no bon, and we lost an awful lot of the boys before we got properly dug in.[19]

Now comes what I reckon was the worst feature of the whole affair. All the stretcher-bearers were killed or wounded and the wounded had to just lie where they were, in some cases for 24 hours on end. It was awful to hear their groans all through that awful day and night. We could not help them as we had to hold the line and there were only a few of us left by now. Our officer and all the NCOs except one in our platoon were either killed or wounded and we were in a bad way, there were so few of us. If Fritz had known he could have wiped us all out then as our rifles would not work – they were jammed with mud, also the machine guns. All that day we held on and the night, also the next day, until the following night when we were relieved after putting in five days and nights in mud up to our knees and without anything to eat or drink except our 24-hours' rations, which we carried with us when going in, and what we could collect from dead men lying round.

However, we got out safely, what was left of us, and a sorry looking lot we were. Some without coats, others without puttees, and most with their clothes all in rags and tatters, and all dead hungry and weary and just tottering with fatigue. The saddest part of all was calling the roll the next day. Since we came out we have been resting, as most of us have very bad feet now and we require a rest badly, also reinforcements, which are arriving daily from England.

Well Lizzie, I will close my letter now, hoping you are all well in NZ as this letter leaves me. Lots of love to all, and I will tell you all a lot more when I return.

I remain, Your Loving Brother,

Ira

In Billets, France
31 OCTOBER 1917

Dear Lizzie,

It is the last day of the month today and it finished up real well as I got no less than twelve letters all together tonight. I will tell you all about it. Yesterday C Company, to which I am attached, walked about six miles in the pouring rain to get a bath and a change of under-clothes. I will tell you about the bath later on, as it may interest you.

Well, after walking six miles there and six back, when we arrived at the billets there was a big bag of NZ mail waiting to be given out. Of course, I reckoned about half of it would be for me as I write an awful lot of letters, although I suppose a good many of them are lost before they reach NZ on account of the submarines etc. I suppose there were three or four hundred letters, and I sat there and waited until the last one was given out and I very near cried when there was not a single one for me. I came home regular down in the dumps and went to bed and slept it off. However, tonight another bag arrived and I got a dozen letters and the other boys had the pleasure of seeing me reading them. There were no less than four of yours among them & I thank you very much for every one of them, and I look forward to seeing the flowers which you send in them as it seems like getting a piece of good old NZ. I am surprised that you have not received more letters from me as I wrote several long ones to each of you from off the boat and no one seems to have received them. Also, I sent PCards to everyone from Cape Town and England. I suppose you will get them all in a heap like I get mine. I don't care, as long as you get them.

I am writing this letter lying in bed with the writing pad on the back of a mirror to make it solid, so if the writing is a bit off, don't blame me. Another thing against good writing is the lice. I have to leave off every now and again and snaffle a few of the most bloodthirsty. Everyone gets lousy after being in France a few weeks, especially if they have not been able to get a change of underclothes regularly. However, as one chap says, these little things are sent to try us and they are better than bullets and HE shells anyway, which is the best way to look at it.[20]

The paper I am writing on came from the Liverpool Fund ChCh, and if it had not been for them I dare say I would not have been able to write to you tonight. We have been exceptionally lucky lately and have received several 'buckshee' parcels, which are very welcome. They usually contain a handkerchief, pair of socks and some tinned stuff, salmon, milk, jam, or coffee or cocoa & milk. I like the cocoa and milk the best of the lot, next to a tin of lollies. We get plenty of tobacco issued free, usually two or three packets of cigarettes each Sunday and a box of matches, so we do all right for smokes, those of us who smoke. I smoke about two cigarettes a week myself now.

I was going to tell you about the bath we had yesterday. We marched six miles in the rain then we were taken in, in lots of twenty, into the bathroom, which was made of canvas and had an iron roof with plenty of air holes in it. After we got in we peeled off our dirty clothes and handed them in to a room in the middle of the bathhouse, also our uniform and boots. Then we were lined up under the showers, and when everyone was in the water was turned on for about half a minute and the fun commences. To begin with there is only about five holes in the shower, and when all is said and done each man gets about a pint and a half of water, nearly boiling. When we are finished we are all as cold as frogs and lose no time in getting our clean clothes and getting in to them. We then marched home and, as it was very cold, rum was issued to those who took it and we imagined we were a wee bit cleaner.

I will have to stop now as the lights are out in a few minutes, so goodbye for tonight.

1 PM, 1 NOVEMBER

Dear Lizzie,

As I am not on parade until 2pm I thought I would put in the spare hour writing a few more lines to you. I was put into the Lewis gun team a few days ago, and this afternoon we are to get some instructions on it as most of us are new men in the team. When I was down at the mail the day before yesterday I saw a lot of letters there for Herbert Harris, Harry Harris' only boy – you remember Herby.[21] I am sorry to say he was killed instantly by a HE shell on the eleventh of Oct. My word, his people will take it very hard, being the only boy.

I told as much as I am allowed to tell about the last advance in which we took part in a previous letter, in fact, I think I told you rather more than I intended to when I began the letter. Anyway, I am not going to tell you anything about the war as you will see far more in the papers than I can ever tell you, even if it is more than half lies. Since the stunt we have been out of the line, what is left of us, resting and training and getting reinforcements from Blighty, of which we are badly in need as we had a lot of men wounded in the advance. The place where we went over is just about as hot as anywhere on the whole front and Fritz does not give way easily, I can assure you.

Well, I don't know I am sure what to write about besides the war, as we know practically nothing about anything else. We seldom see a paper and seem all out of touch with the outside world. That reminds me, I have a new address. It is Rifleman I.G.H.G. Robinson 40846, C. Company, 12th Platoon, 2nd Battalion, New Zealand Rifle Brigade. I have to put the address in the middle of the letter as we are not allowed to put it at the end, why, goodness only knows. Where we are now billeted is in a very pretty part of France.[22] It would suit Joe just down to the ground; in fact, I guess he ought to have been a Froggie as their life would just suit him. To begin with the land is very good and is cut up into very small lots, some only about half an acre, others larger. Five or six acres would be reckoned a large paddock here. Each small lot is held by a different farmer and they make a living off it somehow or other, so you can guess not an inch of it is wasted. It is beautiful to get on the top of a hill and look down and as far as you can see all these small lots, some in crop, some ploughed etc, divided in some cases by hawthorn hedges, but more often only by a shallow drain which forms the boundary. The parts of the hills where they cannot plough are used for grazing purposes, but even these parts are not fenced. Instead of a fence they send a couple of small girls or boys up with the herd, and they keep them off the cultivated plots. Labour here is very cheap whereas fences are dear, like everything else in France. You can travel for hours and hours here along the roads and you will not see a single fence to speak of; perhaps you will see a sort of half pie hawthorn fence round a house or some place like that. The main roads here are very good indeed, as they should be considering the hundreds of years they have been in use. Another thing I noticed was that nearly all the main roads have a row of trees planted along each side; this makes them very pretty, but they have been a good mark for Fritz's artillery during this war as he knows exactly where the roads are by them.

They have very fine horses in France and they think the world of them, and the horses do just as they like and stop and have a rest whenever they like, as far as I can see. They all are as fat as mud and seem about the only thing in France that is well cared for and fed properly. In France you have to have a license to breed horses, which accounts for the high standard that is maintained. A good horse is worth £100 in some parts of France. There is another thing I noticed, and that is there is not a single young chap left on the farms. All the work is done by boys and girls, old men and women. They are up before daylight in the morning and work until they cannot see to work any longer. It is a pitiful, although not uncommon sight, to see a poor old dame, often on the wrong side of fifty, wheeling an enormous load of stuff, straw, hay, beans etc, on a wheelbarrow home after working all day in the fields pulling mangles, carrots etc, and every kind of agricultural work. It is a jolly shame and the people over there have no idea of the effect of the war on the French farmer. We were hoping it would be over this winter, but the events of the last few months have altered things a good deal; but it may be over a lot sooner than we expect all the same.

A great deal of time is wasted on the farms in France by the people being so much behind the times. For instance, in many cases the wheat sheaves are still tied by hand with a whisk of straw, and a few days ago I gave an old man a hand to thresh some wheat with a flail, so my grass-seeding days were not altogether wasted, were they?[23] They also stick to the single furrow plough and mess around with wooden harrows and all that sort of thing. I have not seen a windmill for water-pumping purposes since I arrived in France, but I have seen dozens of huge mills with canvas sails on them which are used for grinding flour, the same as one used to see on Christmas cards years and years ago. Also I have seen dozens of water wheels, also used for milling purposes. They are very slow affairs, but they run continually and grind a lot of flour in a long time. Hot water services are unheard of here and are not missed as they have never been seen. All the houses have a well with a wee house built over it and thatched in most cases with straw etc, with a hand windlass, chain and bucket, the same as a hundred years ago. There is one thing I noticed and that is the stoves. The most of them are placed right out in the room to get all the heat from them. They are nearly all beautifully designed and cast and nearly all have tiled fronts. There are all kinds of them and some are very pretty indeed, others are very old and are very quaint affairs and I am sure you would fall in love with them if you saw them. I did. I wish I could fetch one back to NZ with me, it would be a real novelty there and no mistake. I have also seen several very fine grandfather clocks and I would really like to get hold of one, but they are rather big affairs to carry round with you.

Since I wrote the last page I have been out and helped clean up our gun and now it is ready for another fly at old Fritz but we, the gun team, are not dying to go into action again. They are a wonderful gun, they only weigh about 30 lbs with the magazine on and are capable of firing 700 rounds of ammunition a minute, although it is seldom, if ever, they need to do so in actual warfare. You see I have got back to war again, so I will have to try and rake up something else to write about, although it is no easy job I can assure you, but I am not doing so bad, am I? I don't know what our officer will say when he has to read this and censor it. I guess he will swear a bit.

The writing paper you sent as it happened was not needed badly this time, but at times we are very short and it will come in handy later on for sure, so I would be pleased if you continue to put in a sheet, but envelopes are the worst to get hold of over here as the ones the Froggies use are as big as a Maori kit. I was pleased to hear Uncle Olliver suffered so little before the end. It is a Godsend to pass away like that and I am sure it is the end he would have chosen, and if ever a man was ready to go it was him. I know of no man who led a better or cleaner life. I have not met Percy yet, but I believe he is in billets about 5 miles away, and if I am here on Sunday I will try and look him up and will be sure and deliver your message. Also I will try and get something to send to Mary when we get near a town again. There is absolutely nothing but wine shops here and wine is no use to her, I guess. I was glad to hear Mary was to be married and I hope she will be happy, as she deserves to be if anyone does. As for the cake which you sent, Lizzie, it has not arrived yet, but I hope it will be along soon now as I am just dying for a piece of decent cake, which they don't know how to make in France, I am satisfied. Anyway, thank you for it and I hope it arrives soon. Bella sent me a cake which I received about a week ago and I don't know when I enjoyed anything so much.[24] It has made me cake hungry, anyway. I have received four parcels altogether since I arrived here: two from Isabel, one from Bella, and one from Miss Mackenzie of Taitapu, which came as a great surprise.[25] I know there must be dozens on the way somewhere and I ought to get some soon.

I think I have been colder than ever you have been or are likely to get, as I was wet to the knees for five days and nights in the stunt and I never felt my feet all the time; but since I have come out they are very painful, as they were half frozen and the blood is just beginning to flow naturally in them again now after about three weeks. I hope you will never get as bad as that, as it is no joke. Some of the boys are in hospital with their feet and it will be months before they are right again.

The papers have not arrived yet but I believe they are sent by a slower boat and very likely will arrive with the parcels. I will stop now Lizzie, and I must thank you for writing so often, as I know you have written even if I don't receive all of your letters, and another thing I would like to say is that I write as often as I can, at least once a fortnight, sometimes twice, and good long letters too.[26]

Dear Lizzie,

Here it is, nearly the end of the year and the war still goes on. I
am beginning to think it will never end, but I hope I am wrong. What
ever possessed Dad to come up and stay with you? I guess he must
be getting quite lively in his old age. Anyway, the change will do
you both good and will break the monotony a little, for you
especially.

I had a great piece of luck the other day as I was sent back to this
camp, which is a training camp a good way back from the line,
instead of going in again as I expected to do. Just a few of us came
back, so I was indeed lucky. The camp is very decent as we have huts
to live in instead of tents, and a good job too as the weather is now
getting very cold; in fact, we had a slight fall of snow and sleet last
night. It was very cold, I can assure you, but luckily I had plenty of
blankets and did not notice it until I turned out in the morning. We
also have a decent YMCA here where we can get a cup of cocoa for a
penny and can also buy any amount of biscuits, salmon and other
tinned stuff, and also they arrange concerts for the boys nearly every
night; if not a concert, a debate or something else to interest us.[27]
Then there is a military band here, in fact, our own 2nd Battalion
band, which is reckoned to be one of the best in France, so we have
plenty of music anyway. Each battalion has a band of its own, and
altogether there are about 16 bands attached to the NZ forces in
France. I guess it would surprise a good many people in NZ to know
that. The soldiers and officers usually bag the instruments and there

are always plenty of players among us as it is a real good job. As a rule bandsmen do not go in to the front line with the rest of the boys. There are also two shops in the camp, run by Froggies, where we can buy anything in the way of sweets or coffee. Before I finish about the band I would like to mention that Pat Cole from Lyttelton is conductor of the best one and is now a 1st Lieutenant, so it is all right to be a bandsman sometimes. I had a long talk with him not long ago and got him to censor a letter for me. Funny how things change, isn't it? Also, we are within a couple of miles of a decent town, which we can get leave to visit, but I have not been in there yet as my funds have run out until payday, four days hence. After payday I am going to buy and send to you a book called 'The New Zealander at the Front', and will also get one for Mary Olliver as I have not sent anything to her yet. I would like to send one to each of you, but the blooming things cost $3^1/_2$ francs each and francs are scarce in France, I can assure you. I hope you receive them all right, as I am sure a good many things have gone astray.

I received one parcel from you and Ada, the one with the sardines, soap & saccharin tablets etc, and I must thank you very much for it. Everything in it was very acceptable, I can assure you. About those badges for the girls: I sent them back from Sling, also the set of buttons, NZR etc, which were on my tunic when I arrived there. I hope you have got them by now as I would not like you to lose them. The ones for you I put in a small parcel by themselves. The ones I sent to Dulcie were in another parcel, much bigger, as there was a collection of about one hundred of them altogether, also some books and postcards – views of London etc.

Some time ago we put in seven days in one of old Fritz's bivvies, and perhaps it would interest you to know what they are like.[28] To begin with they were built by the Germans to accommodate their soldiers and shelter them from the snow, bullets and pieces of shells. They use in the first place huge sheets of corrugated steel, made in curved sheets a quarter the circumference of a circle. Looking at the edge of one of them they look like this:

Now they put two of these together like this

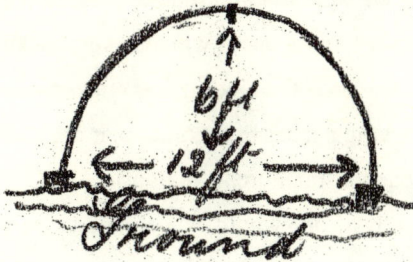

forming a half circle of iron or steel. They put enough iron up to make a bivvie about 15 ft or more long, according to what is required. After fixing the iron securely in position they set to work and covered the whole affair with about four or five feet of concrete, reinforced with bars of iron, railway rails and barbed wire, in fact, any pieces of iron that they could find. On top of this they piled heaps of logs, sticks and any rubbish that was lying about, making the whole look like a heap of rubbish. The ends were finished off with a wall of concrete about three feet thick, and a small door is left in one end, which is the only ventilation there is to the place. The ends are then covered with logs and rubbish, and I can tell you it is very hard to see one, even when close to them. Nothing but a direct hit will smash one of them up, and when I tell you the one we were in had been shelled by both our guns and Fritz's for months, you will see it is exceptionally hard to hit one of them. We put seven days in one and he put hundreds of shells all round us but never hit the bivvie once, but he knocked a wee bit off the corner. If you are in one and a shell lands anywhere near, it shakes the ground like an earthquake and is not too pleasant, I can assure you. However, we lived through it all, although it was a bit crowded as there were fifteen of us in a place about sixteen feet long and twelve feet wide. Some crowd, eh? We were not allowed out at all in the daytime and had to do all our work in the dark, which is very awkward. I suppose you wonder how we fared for food. It was cooked miles back from the lines, and carrying parties brought it up at night. We used to get cooked meat & bacon, soup, bread, margarine, cheese and jam, so did not fare so badly as one would expect, and twice a week rum was issued to those who wanted it. Nearly all, you bet! As we were not allowed to light a fire we had to be content with water to drink, that is when we could not boil our dixies on the sly when no one was about to see us.[29]

Well Lizzie, I will have to stop now as a chap wants to shout me a cup of cocoa and I don't want to miss it as it is very cold tonight, so I will conclude with love to you all in old NZ.

I remain, Your Loving Brother,

Ira

P.S. Please send letter on. Love to all.

P.P.S. Hope you can read this. It is too long to read again and correct.

France
19 DECEMBER 1917

Dear Lizzie,

I received your letter of 23 Sept tonight, and as I have a few
minutes to spare before the lights go out I am going to start a letter
in reply. You speak as if you had not had many letters from me, but I
can only assure you, as I have done often before, I have written
dozens of letters and I hope before now you will have received some
of them, also the badges which I sent to the girls. I will have to stop
now as it is too cold to sit up in bed writing, so I will stop until
another time.

20 DECEMBER

I am going to write a bit more tonight, but it is a bit of a job. I
have to lie on my stomach on my bed and write on my pillow, a
sandbag full of straw, with a candle balanced on the top of a tin of
honey, which I received from Isabel today. I don't know I am sure
what to write about, but I am not going to write about the war, which
has been going all wrong lately and the less said about it the better. I
suppose I will have to fall back on the weather.

The winter up till now, I am told, has been very mild, but we had
a fall of snow, a very slight one, two day ago and I can assure you it
was plenty cold enough for me, even if others said it was mild. Do
you know what I wear? A thick undershirt, a woollen shirt, a
cardigan, my tunic, a leather jerkin and a pair of gloves, and if it is
blowing cold, an overcoat as well, and then I am not too warm. I can
tell you, when I get my Webb equipment on top and a good load of

ammunition up I can hardly toddle along and I guess I look a bit of a hard doer, but as all the rest are the same I suppose I am not conspicuous.

I say, such a funny thing happened last Monday. I was working on a fatigue job building new huts for the NZ boys' winter quarters, and as it was a very cold day I dodged behind a few sheets of iron out of the wind. I had not been there long when who should walk round the corner but Percy Olliver, and I can tell you we had a great old yarn and I went into his hut and had a good warm at a decent fire. He is in the orderly room and so far he has been very lucky and has not had a single day's illness since he joined up.

I suppose by now you know that Herbert Harris and, I think, Jack Ware were killed at Passchendaele, but I managed to get through the lot without a scratch. I am not sure about Jack Ware, but I think he is gone all right.[30] Poor little Alex Grey, the schoolmaster from Akaroa who only arrived two days before the stunt, was also wounded, how badly I do not know; also Jack Hayward from Akaroa, who was my mate until he got his smack and went to hospital. I had such a nice letter from Bob Ellison a few weeks ago. He tells me his eldest son is going to German E. Africa and the next one, Eric, is an orderly in the Walton-on-Thames Hospital as his heart is weak and he is not fit for active service in France. Lucky devil.

Just fancy, in another five days it will be Christmas Day & we are all to get a regular flash dinner for which we put in a couple of francs each. I suppose it would surprise the people in NZ to know that we all put in two francs a fortnight to help buy rations, as what they supply us with is not sufficient, and then they talk about how well we are treated compared with the Tommy. It is all bunkum. Our battalion came out of the line about ten days ago, and we are supposed to be out until after Christmas if all goes well and old Fritz does not make himself a nuisance in the meantime. I was not in the line with them last time. I was away down at a training camp and I may have some news for you next time I write. That reminds me, my address, which I must put in the middle of my letter, is 40846, Rifleman I.G.H.G. Robinson, C. Company, 12 Platoon, 2nd Battalion, New Zealand Rifle Brigade, France.

I was pleased to hear Joe did so well up in the country, as I guess you can do with all your money these times, if things are as dear over there as they are here. Do you know what I paid for a tea of two eggs, a piece of steak and some potato chips, and a cup of tea, no pudding of any sort, only two pieces of bread and butter? Five francs, which in English money is equal to about 4/2. Pretty hot, isn't it? I guess you are better off in NZ.

I was pleased to hear the children were getting on all serene and that you were better also, and if you take my advice have as good a time as you can. There is no reason why you should not go out for an evening occasionally, as I know Joe would like to see you go out more than you do. I know you have not had much of a time, but if you saw what the poor people over here have gone through you would begin to think you were lucky. Only today we passed through a town which Fritz had shelled to pieces. At one time there used to be over 30,000 of a population, now there are none at all and the whole town is absolutely smashed to pieces. There are hardly two bricks left on top of one another. It is awful to think of the damage done to an un-offending people who are now homeless and ruined.

I will have to stop now as it is late and I am half frozen, so goodbye, with love to yourself and Joe and the children and all the rest in NZ.

I remain, Your Loving Brother,

Jha

France

28 JANUARY 1918

Dear Lizzie,

I received a letter from you today, also several a few days ago, and as I have a bit of time to spare this evening I am going to answer them. Today I also received three parcels, one from Isabel and two others, one a tin of chocolates and the other a tin of condensed milk. I do not know who sent the milk and chocolate as it did not say on the outside and it is hard to pick writing on cloth, but whoever it was – and I guess it was you – I thank very much for sending the parcels; also Ira Petterson, who I see sent the parcel from Le Bons Bay.[31] I can assure you sweets and milk are always appreciated over here as it is very hard to get decent sweets in France. As for milk, they make nothing over here to compare with the milk made in NZ.

In one way I was pleased to hear Bob had gone in to camp and I was not a bit surprised to hear it as we are very short of men over here. It will do him good if he gets through all right and it is my opinion that he will be just in time to see the end. I don't think the war will last longer than this winter, as each side has had quite enough of it long ago and both are now waiting to see which will give in. It is dead funny, neither can beat the other and both want to dictate peace terms to the other. Great, isn't it? I don't think Bob will stand the work we have to do over here anyway, and I hope he will land a good job before he reaches the firing line. I, too, am glad Mother is not here to see both Bob and I go to the war as it would have been the death of her, and it is better she does not need to worry over it now. I don't think they will call up very many more men in NZ and I will tell you why. The NZ Division in France is composed of four brigades, and a few weeks ago they decided to do away with the 4th Brigade and use the men to reinforce the other three brigades and the Pioneer Battalion. I myself am quite satisfied that NZ has done more than her share in this war and I think what men she has now should stay where they are, otherwise the country will be ruined for want of labour. The French have taken a tumble to the situation and now give their men plenty of leave on condition that they put so much time in working on their farms.

It seems funny to me to hear you speaking, or at least writing, of holidays, show week etc. We do not know what a holiday is over here and work Sunday, Monday and all the rest of the days and a good part of the nights as well. If it was not for payday we would not know the day or date and it would not be long before we would not know the month we were in, either.

I was pleased to hear Joe had been doing so well and I hope he will continue to do so as I guess the money is all needed just now, if things are as dear over there as they are here. I was pleased to know that you got the PC of Folkestone all right, and I hope the others got theirs too, as I sent some cards all round. As you say, it is a very pretty place and in normal times I guess one could have a right royal good time there. We stayed there a day on the way over and enjoyed ourselves fine. We started off by having a good meal, then a good bath, followed by a good look over the town, which included a visit to the fish market that amused me all to pieces. The fishermen fetch their catch in and sell it themselves and I can tell you there is not half a racket, all hands talking at once and no one listening. They catch and sell anything, even flounders not more than three inches long. The fishing boats there are usually rather big ones with oil engines in them, and nearly all are armed with quick-firing guns ready to deal with any tin fish that may come along and annoy them.

My word, you are coming out of your shell and no mistake, but I think it is a good idea your learning to ride a bike as you can slip round so quickly on one when once you have learned to ride it, which is not a very hard job. I knew Herbert Harris was killed, he was killed instantly by a HE shell the night before we went over at Passchendaele. I got full particulars about it and wrote a short note to his father giving him all details as far as I knew them. Poor old Herby, I never thought I would be fighting in this hell of a country with him. He was in the same company as I am, he was 11 Platoon, I am in 12 Platoon. The same day or the next Jack Ware was wounded, and I hear he is now on his way back to NZ after being only about one week in France. Pretty rough going, isn't it?

Since I wrote to you last we have had another turn in the front line and I am glad to say I managed to scramble through once again without being hit or injured in any way. The weather was simply rotten and we had a very miserable six days in there. First of all it snowed, then it rained and melted the snow and caused the sides of the trenches to fall in, and then the men walking up and down churned it all in to mud which reached nearly to our waists. It was awful, you have no idea what it was like, and for a whole week we never had our gumboots off except to change our socks either night or day. The wet also caused our bivvies to fall in and we had no sleep at all for several days. There was only one consolation, and that was old Fritz's trenches are in lower country than ours and he must be having a worse time than us. In the end our trenches got that bad we could not walk in them, so we took to the open country on top and if we wanted to go anywhere we hopped out and ran for it and gave old Fritz some good sniping. He only got a couple of our boys all the time we were messing about there, so we were lucky and no mistake.

Well Lizzie, I will close my letter now as it is late, so goodbye for the present and I will write again soon. Love to all in dear old NZ.

I remain, Your Loving Brother,

Ira

France

16 MARCH 1918

Dear Lizzie,

I received a parcel of sweets from you two days ago, posted on 9 January, and as I am off this afternoon I thought it would be a good chance to write and thank you for sending it. I don't expect I will be able to finish this letter, but anyway I can start it.

We are in a camp now near Ypres and we are doing fatigue work behind the line and in the support lines. We work mostly at night as old Fritz has a nasty habit of shelling us if we show ourselves too much in the day time. I was supposed to go out on this afternoon's fatigue, but it was rumoured that Sir Douglas Haig was going to visit us and so we were kept back to form a guard or something or other.[32] I hope he does not come and then I will have a decent afternoon off to do a bit of writing as I am all behind with my correspondence. This is a rotten camp where we are now, although the huts etc are good. There is a battery of naval guns, four of them, all round the camp, and when they open fire the noise is something tremendous and the concussion nearly shakes the huts to pieces. They fire mostly at night, so you can guess how much sleep we get when we do get a chance to go to bed. It would not be so bad if the shells all went over to Fritz, but he sends a few back as well. Last night our guns opened out on him and just by way of retaliation he sent over about 600 gas shells in the hope of gassing the guns' crews. However, he did not do it as our guns pelted him with 9 inch shells the whole night through. I don't think he caught anyone, although all his shells lobbed within a few hundred yards of our camp.

82

Lots of people think there is only one kind of gas and only one way in which it is used, but that is not so. Cloud gas, which the public knows most about, is not used nearly so much now as it used to be, for two reasons, or perhaps three. The first is because it takes weeks to prepare to deliver a gas attack and in that time the whole concern may be shelled to pieces. The second is because of the expense. The third is that the gas does not usually reach the guns in the rear, which after all are the chief fighting factors in the war. Old Fritz & our heads as well soon realized this & were not long finding a new way of sending it over, namely in shells, which can be landed right amongst the guns and are very deadly, as our artillery men have found out many a time. Now for the different kinds of gas. First of all there is a tear shell gas, which as its name implies causes the eyes to shed buckets of tears so that you cannot see what you are doing or where you are going. Then there is a gas which makes you sneeze, and old Fritz send this over mixed with other gasses in the hope that it will make you sneeze and be unable to put on your respirator quickly. Then there is another gas which affects the heart and lungs and which is the worst of the whole bunch. And last but not least, mustard gas, which he sends over in liquid form and which causes a blister like a scald wherever it gets on you and is no bon, although it is not considered a very dangerous gas, but all the same I don't want any of it. The worst part about it is that the gas remains in the shell hole for days after, and if you duck into the hole for shelter it will blister your hands and any parts which it touches, and if your clothes are not changed it will gradually work through them and blister the skin underneath. However, enough about gas or you will be thinking I am going to be gassed or something else, although I have never on any occasion had to wear my respirator yet and hope I never will as they are anything but comfortable, even if they are better than old Fritz's ones.

Before we came to this camp we were away back at a place called Moulle where the whole Rifle Brigade did a week's shooting.[33] We have to do a week's shooting every now & again to keep us in practice, as sometimes we do not fire a shot for weeks on end. Funny sort of war, isn't it? Round Moulle the country was very beautiful, and as I have said before is just like a big garden made up of hundreds of small plots divided by ditches, etc. Each plot is composed of five or six acres and is reckoned a farm in France. Some plots have just been ploughed, in others the crops are just beginning to come through, while in others they are five or six inches high. It looks like a huge draughtboard, the squares being composed of every imaginable shade of green, with every here and there a red brick homestead with a pink tiled roof and on nearly every rise a huge windmill with brown sails set, which seem to turn continually.

From Moulle we marched to a small station where we entrained and passed through some very interesting country, which I will try and tell you about. To begin with it is very low lying and to drain it, as well as for another reason, the people, Froggies not Belgians, have cut channels about ten feet wide and about six or seven feet deep, which have about four feet of clear, peaceful water in them. Here again the whole country is cut into smallholdings, but they differ from around Moulle in that they are all in long, narrow strips with a channel on each side which acts as a fence, boundary & road. The plots are usually about 2 chains wide and about 10 long and are nearly all used for the cultivation of vegetables for different large towns close by.

Here again is seen all sorts of crops in all stages and the whole looks very pretty indeed. As you can see, a horse and cart would be of no use in a place like this on account of the channels, so they use boats. Imagine a Froggie with his wife & children, usually about six or seven, in the bow of his boat, with a background of cabbages and pumpkins etc, and the Froggie himself acting skipper in the stern with a long oar with which he propels the whole turnout. The people all seem happy and contented there, although the guns can be heard roaring away in the distance and there is not a young man to be seen who is not in uniform. Of course, the channels between the plots lead into and join larger and deeper ones, which in turn join large canals up and down which huge barges glide, full of stuff which the smaller boats have brought down to them. The canals run all through the country and eventually reach the sea. Along their banks are built the towns & villages, which in some cases are very pretty indeed, with their funny old swing bridges and quaintly dressed people.

I think this is all I will have time to write today as it is now getting on for tea time and if I am not in the first wave of the big push I will miss for sure. I saw Percy Olliver again a week or two ago and he is still going strong and looks real well. We happened to both be getting water from an old Fritz well when we met. Funny, wasn't it, when there were hundreds at the well all day long, and I came from a pillbox half a mile away and had no idea that he was even in the same sector. I will try and write some more tomorrow if I get a chance.

18 MARCH

As I thought, I did not finish my letter the other day so I am going to try and do so today. Yesterday an NZ mail came in and I got about fourteen letters, among them being a couple from you, one dated way back in September, so it must have gone astray somewhere on the way over. The other one from you was dated 8 Jan, and as I have had several in between, the September one must certainly have had a good cruise round. Several of the other ones were also dated September. Goodness only knows where they have been in the meantime – I don't. Anyway, I was glad to get them, even if they were a bit late in coming. Better luck next time, I hope.

Now I am stuck for news once again. What in the wide world shall I write about? We know nothing, hear nothing, see nothing but the war, and only that which takes place in our sector which is only one little part in a front hundreds of miles long, so it is no joke trying to write a letter leaving out the war, about which the less said the better. I think I will have to give up writing for today as I am dead tired, and I will explain why. Yesterday we walked about six miles to do fatigue, put in eight hours, walked six miles home, getting home at about 8pm, and by the time we had tea it was bedtime. However, we did not get any sleep as Fritz shelled our camp all night long until we had to turn out at 4.30am this morning and do another eight hours' fatigue in the same place as yesterday. It was no bon, I can tell you, and the boys are all dead tired and grumpy and are lying asleep all over the place.

I think I will have to stop now, so I will conclude by asking you to ask plenty of questions when you write, about anything and everything. I will ring off now, with love to all in good old New Zealand.

I remain, Your Loving Brother,

Ira

France
12 A<small>PRIL</small> 1918

Dear Lizzie,

Before I go very far with this letter I must warn you that it will
not be a very long one as I am writing it under rather trying
conditions, as I will explain later. I received your last two letters
dated January while we were in the front line trenches and I am
answering them from the same place, sitting on my steel hat with the
lid of a bomb box on my knee for a writing desk and old Fritz
shelling all the time, but he is sending them well over so they are not
worrying us much. He is shelling two towns well behind the lines. I
am going to send this letter in a round about way, so you can just do
a bit of guessing as to how it arrived and I will tell you next time I
write.

As you very likely know by now we are in a new sector near
Amiens, a big railway centre in the north of France, and I will tell
you how we got here. We were doing fatigue work behind the line up
in the Ypres sector, and having a pretty rough time into the bargain,
when all of a sudden we got word to pack up in the middle of the
night as we were going to shift in a hurry somewhere, we did not
know where. Well, we marched out of that camp and after walking
most of the night we reached another camp near the railway and the
town of Poperinghe. There we rested all one day and those who had
not made wills were compelled to make one out. The following, or at
least the same night, we packed up and marched out again, and after
walking two or three miles we entrained and started on an all night
ride. It was not by any means a pleasant one as we were told off in

87

lots of thirty and bundled into covered vans and told to make ourselves as comfortable as possible on the floor. It was one tangled mass of legs, arms, boots, rifles and equipment, steel hats and gas helmets, but in spite of all that I managed to get a few hours' sleep. I can sleep on a brick now and not even get a little bit stiff. The only . thing that would keep me awake would be a decent bed, which I have not seen for months and months.

We travelled all that night and the next day we arrived at Amiens, where we detrained and had a meal and a rest in a park just out of the town. In passing, I think I will describe the streets of Amiens which are very beautiful indeed, that is the main streets. On the side of the street there is a row of beautiful trees, then a footpath, then another row of trees, then a roadway with a tramline running along it; but the trams have not been running for months and months, the men being all away at the war and the coal etc being wanted for war purposes. The war is no joke in France, I can tell you. Then we have another row of trees and then another footpath, then more trees, then another roadway, then more trees and a footpath and lastly another row of trees. As you may guess, the streets are very wide and are arranged something like this:

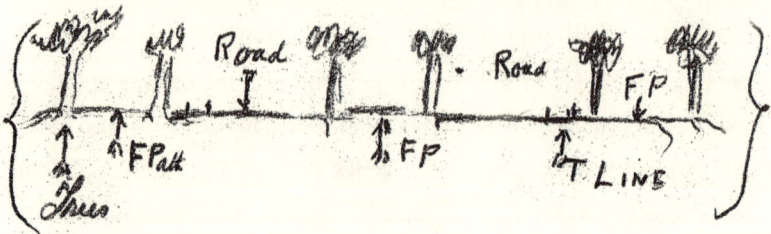

Hope you can follow the sketch.

The winning Rifle Drill Squad, Tauherenikau Military Sports. Ira Robinson seated on chair, first left, middle row. See letter dated 6 February 1917, page 17.

The 23rd Reinforcements' route march over the Rimutakas, 1917. See letter written 'At Sea' April 1917, page 23.

*No. 31 Platoon resting during the 23rd Reinforcements'
route march over the Rimutakas, 1917. Ira Robinson second
from right, front row. See letter written 'At Sea' April 1917,
page 23.*

*Paperknife and matchbox cover made in the trenches by Ira
Robinson from the propeller of an Allied plane which
crashed near Colincamps, as described in letter dated 20
May 1918, page 94.*

*Convalescing patients at Hornchurch Hospital, England.
Ira Robinson second from right, back row. See letters dated
28 November and 2 December 1918, pages 125 and 127.*

Ira Robinson's wife Sarah Isabella (née Gibson), c. 1920.

Ira and Bella Robinson with their daughters Enid (holding Chrissie) and Shirley, Christchurch, New Years' Day 1951.

Christchurch Home Guard Parade, 1944. Ira Robinson second from right, row nearest camera.

Lizzie Baldwin (née Robinson) on right, with Lizzie Rosewarne, Henderson, c. 1935–40.

Ira Robinson with his granddaughter Chrissie, Christchurch, 1954.

We rested in Amiens all that day and in the middle of the night we were bundled into motor lorries, after having dumped our blankets & overcoats, and away we went in battle order: that is rifle, ammunition, equipment, gas helmet, steel hat and iron rations, and bayonet ready to meet old Fritz, which we were to do sooner than I expected. We travelled some twelve or fourteen miles in the lorries, then we had to get out and walk about another five miles, by which time it was early morning and we were all dead tired and cold, to an open paddock where our cookers were. There we rested for three hours and had a hot meal, which we badly needed. We then got a clean pair of socks each and took off the soiled ones, then we packed up and away we went again. I, for one, began to think that we must be very near the eastern front, but we did not have to go far. After a short walk we reached a village which the people had already left, and were informed that old Fritz was waiting for us on the other side of it. Then, and not till then, did we realise that Fritz had broken through and completely routed or killed or captured the Tommies who were supposed to hold this front, and that the NZ Division, unsupported by one single gun, were the only soldiers between Fritz and the huge town of Amiens, one of the biggest towns and railway centres in France. I forgot to mention that we saw dozens of poor farmers, with as much of their worldly belongings as they could stack on their carts, toiling slowly along the road away from the advancing Huns. It was a heart-rending sight I can assure you, especially to see the poor old women staggering along with huge baskets strapped to their bent shoulders and perhaps pushing a pram full of stuff or else carrying a cat or dog in their arms. Man, it made regular savages of our boys and Fritz has paid the price since.

We stayed in the village about an hour, then we marched through it spread out in three lines in artillery formation and advanced to meet the Hun, which we did about half a mile from the village. We drove him back about a mile and a half, and then we had to halt as it was dark and we were just about done. During the night we consolidated our position, and except in a few places where we advanced, we hold the same line still, in spite of the fact that he has made several attempts to come over and beat us back. All things considered it was a good performance, when you consider that we had not one single piece of artillery to help us along and Fritz had absolutely hundreds of machine guns. Since we came up here we have captured over a hundred of them. We had two of our own to help us when we went over.

However, we stopped him, which is the main thing after all, and I hear there is a great piece in the Paris papers praising the N. Zealanders and thanking them for saving the town of Amiens. We are still in this sector and have been in the front line or supports all the time and goodness knows when we will get relieved – soon, I hope. I am proud of the fact that the Rifle Brigade led the attack and that our battalion, the second, was the first to go over the top. Of course we lost a lot of good men and also officers, but not as many as one might expect under the circumstances, and we have been reinforced a good deal since and are now stronger than ever. So far I thank God I have not received a scratch, although five of my mates were killed by one shell and I was standing in the middle of them, so you see your prayers are not in vain after all. This last stint has made me very bitter towards Fritz and I will never think of him as anything but a savage again and will treat him as such. I am on a gun capable of firing 700 shots a minute and if it would fire 1400 shots a minute it would not be going too quickly for me. I did not intend to write so much when I started but somehow I feel I could write a lot today, but I think I have told you a little too much as it is, so I had better stop.

Isabel in her last letter asks what has become of my stripes, so I will tell her. I handed them in before we left England as no one but a fool would hold what we call buckshee stripes, that is stripes given in NZ. Imagine the position of an N.C.O. who is in the firing line for the first time, being in charge of a party of men, some of whom have been over here in the line fighting two or three years. It is a position impossible to me, anyway, which is why I returned my stripes, one of which I am still entitled to wear if I chose to do so. However, that was months ago, and if the Fourth Brigade had not been broken up to reinforce the other brigades I would probably have had my two stripes back again, but I am not anxious for them, as a plain Rifleman with a whole skin will do me a treat and I sincerely hope the whole business will soon be over.

I received a letter from Dulcie, Ada, Isabel and Willie along with yours and I will answer them later on. I have not the time just now, to say nothing of the opportunity. I have not met Kim Muirson yet and I just missed Willie Muirson by a whisker, I am sorry to say. I was helping to carry out a wounded man when who should I see but Jack McLean, Stella's one-time boy. He had met Will and told me where he was but when I went across to see him, only a few chains away, his company had shifted. A rotten piece of luck, wasn't it? Jack is not looking at all well and looks thin and miserable. He has been over here too long – it gets on one's nerves after a time.

I say, about those badges. I tell you what to do with them. I don't want them, so you girls can divide them amongst yourselves, that is the five of you, including, of course, Stella and Dulcie, who have both been like an extra sister to me since I left NZ. If you don't like to divide them, which I think would be best, you can leave them complete and draw lots for them. In fact, do whatever you like with them, I am easy about it. I received a parcel of honey from Isabel a few days ago and I thank her very much for sending it, and I hope the other parcels will soon arrive as I am looking forward to those biscuits and shortbread.

I will now conclude with love to all in good old NZ, which I hope to see again before many months have passed away.

I remain, Your Loving Brother,

Jha

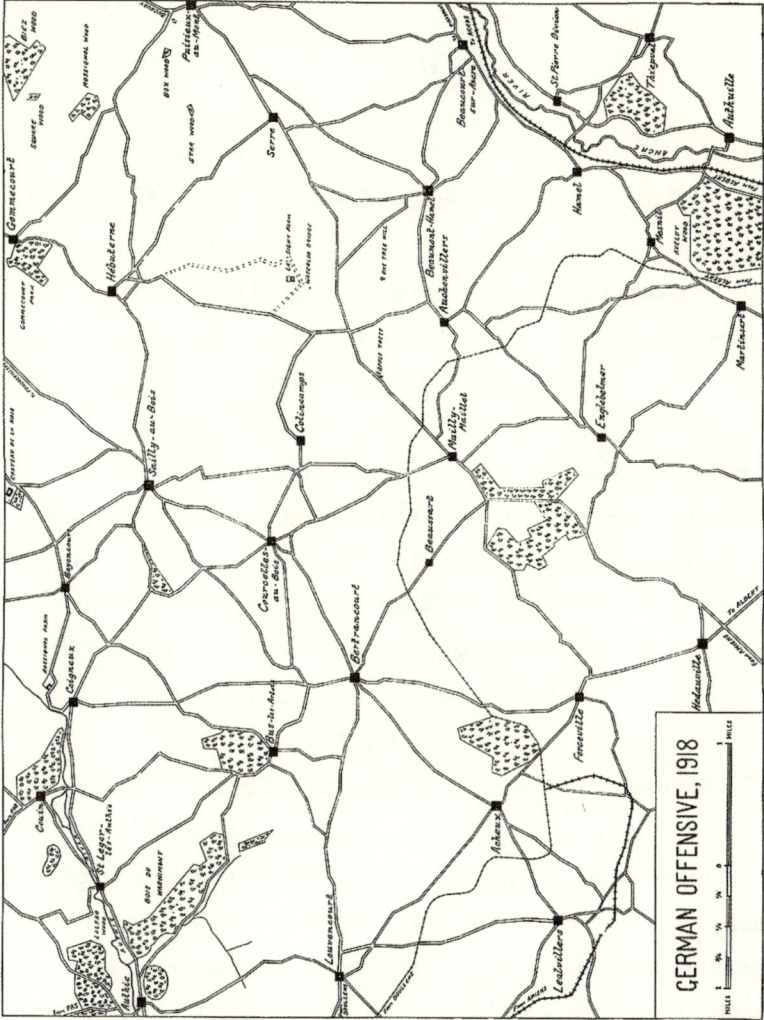

GERMAN OFFENSIVE, 1918

From The History of
the Canterbury
Regiment N.Z.E.F.
1914–1919,
*Captain David
Ferguson, M.C.,
Whitcombe and Tombs,
Auckland, 1921.*

93

France
20 May 1918

Dear Lizzie,

I received a letter and a parcel from you yesterday and as I am off today, or at least this afternoon – we were on fatigue work this morning, digging trenches as usual – I thought I would start a letter to you, but I don't know whether I will be able to finish it or not as I suppose there will be something to do later on.

As you have very likely seen in the newspapers in NZ, we are in a new sector now and I will tell you about it later on.[34] First of all I must thank you for the parcel which you sent. It was a tin of lollies with a note in saying they were from Bob, but as I don't know Bob's address or whether he has left NZ or not yet I cannot write to him, so if you write I would like you to tell him I received the parcel all serene and thank him for sending it. Later on I am going to write a letter to him and address it to the Base Post Office, London, and it is almost sure to find him as soon as he reaches England. The letter which I received from you also had in it a book of YMCA tickets, for which I thank you very much. They are just about the handiest thing one can have in France, better even than this rotten French paper money, which is an awful nuisance to get changed as we get paid in five, ten & twenty franc notes and change is very scarce in France at the present time. However, Lizzie, I don't want you to spend money on me, as I guess you can do with it all yourself now that everything is so dear.

You mentioned in one of your letters, or I think it was Ada, about a Lieut Luke, one of the Miss Taylor's husband. I suppose you know by now that he is on his way back to NZ with shell shock and a wound in the head. He was attached to Coy HQ, and they were bivvied in a cellar in a village called Colincamps when a big nine-inch shell landed fair on top of it and blew it in, killing about a dozen of the HQ staff and General Fulton and Major Purdy.[35] I was there a few minutes after it happened, but I did not know that Lieut Luke was in the cellar. He must have got out and been sent away before the party who came to dig out any who were alive – and to which I belonged – arrived, as we were a wee while on the way because we had to hunt up shovels etc, and it was raining like mad and pitch dark. It was in the same village only a few chains away that five of my mates were killed all with one shell, three of them being on our gun team. I had a letter from Robert Ellison and he was telling me about Luke going back to NZ.

I had a bit of bad luck the other day. I had hunted round until I had quite a collection of odds and ends of German stuff such as a piece of machine gun belt with empty cartridges in it, a clip of Fritz cartridges, some buttons and tassel off a Hun bayonet, and I packed them all up and was going to send them to you, and the bounders would not let them go through the post office and sent them back to me. I was not half wild, as I had spent quite a while packing them up and sewing a cover round them and getting the officer to censor them for me. What objection they can have to our sending a few trifles home like that I don't know. More red tape! Red tape is the only thing that does not seem to have run short since the war began. I wish it would run a bit short and then perhaps we might finish the war. As one Blighty paper aptly puts it, last year we did not win the war on account of the mud, and this year we will not win it on account of the muddle. However, I hope they are wrong as I think everyone has had enough of it by now, and I guess old Fritz is sorry he ever started this tangi.

We were in reserve near Colincamps, and as I had a good deal of time on my hands – we were supposed to show ourselves as little as possible during the day – I carved a paperknife and posted it to you. It has rather a history attached to it. When we came up here first we carried very little, not even our overcoats, as we were doing forced marches all the way and were carrying extra ammunition and bombs etc. Well, we arrived at Colincamps and found Fritz in possession, but only a very few of them. We drove them out and away past the village to where the front line now is, a matter of a couple of miles or so, where there were thousands of Fritzes and we could not go any further. We remained there until relieved a few days later, and as it was very cold and wet and we had no overcoats we collected a Fritz one each and there we were, more like Fritzes than New Zealanders. When we were relieved we came back to Colincamps, fetching our souvenir overcoats with us, of course. While we were in there an airman in one of our latest planes had trouble with his engine and had to land in a field just outside the village. Seeing the plane land our chaps grew curious and took a stroll over – wearing the Hun coats – and the poor airman, mistaking them for the real thing in Huns, got the wind up, set the plane on fire and took to his scrapers. The airmen call us mud wallopers, but that joker walloped mud just about as quick as I have ever seen any man, and I don't blame him either. The plane was all burned except the iron work, engine etc, and the propeller, and the paperknife is made of a piece of one of the blades which I hacked off one day with my bayonet as I was passing. The rest of the boys reckoned it was rather good and I hope you get it all right. I can tell you it took some making with only an old blunt jackknife.

I have also a little piece of brass which I have made into a pendant, and when I get a chance I will post it back to NZ to Harry. It also has a history. It is made of a piece of copper which I got out of a disabled tank in the Ypres sector while we were building strong points up there in March, and I have carried it with me all through this last stunt. I am also going to try and send an aluminium matchbox cover back for Winston: it is made of a piece of the same plane as the paperknife. They are only trifles, but are all we are allowed to send, and then we cannot always get them away. When we get off the line again (???) and are somewhere near a town or village, I may be able to get something to send the other children. At present the towns near us are deserted and in ruins, and what the Froggies have not taken away has been smashed to pieces by shell fire etc. It is an awful shame, I don't think ever there was such a hellish war. It is wicked the way whole beautiful towns and villages have been absolutely ruined.

We are just beginning to get beautiful summer, or at least spring, weather here now, and today it is glorious, beautiful sunshine and a nice cool breeze. The whole country round here is simply lovely and the fields, except where they are pockmarked by huge shell holes, are just one mass of colour – yellow and blue and white and greens of all shades. In peacetime this must have been a most beautiful place indeed, and the Froggies have assisted nature by planting thousands of trees in all their towns and along the sides of the roads. There are hundreds of miles of them. The Ypres sector is quite different to this place, as the fighting has been worse and the ground has been blown to pieces for feet down and there is not a blade of grass to be seen and all the trees are dead or smashed to pieces or blown clean out by the roots. Do you know, within six feet of our bivvie there is cocksfoot grass up to my knees, and every time I look at it it reminds me of the bays; and our trench zigzags in and out among a group of beautiful trees just looking their best, and if it was not for the continual scream of the shells going over to Fritz and the thud of his bursting in a village close by, it would be more like a picnic than a war.

I think it is a good joke, too, about the song book on the march stunt, and I can assure you we don't have much breath to spare for singing on this side of the world. All our spare breath as far as I can see is used up swearing at the cobbles, the officers and the whole outfit generally.

I have not seen Percy Olliver again, and goodness only knows when I will, as all our troops are in the line now and we only see one another as we change over, and perhaps we may not relieve his company for months. In fact, it is only a mere fluke if we do happen to meet at any time. I cannot understand why the buttons and badges did not reach you safely, as I posted them from Sling Camp before I left England. I suppose some rotter in the PO pinched them. Never mind, it cannot be helped I suppose, but it is a nark.

I will have to stop now as this is my last sheet of paper. Anyway, I have not done so bad considering I am living in a trench with nothing but grass etc and barbed wire entanglements to look at all day long, so I will say goodbye with love to all.

I remain, Your Loving Brother,

Ira

P.S. Received two letters from Dulcie and will answer them as soon as possible. Am waiting for news.

France
5 June 1918

Dear Lizzie,

We are having a sort of a holiday until 4pm today from dinner time so I thought I would just write you a few lines, if I can keep awake long enough. We have just had dinner and I could go to sleep like one thing as it is a sleepy sort of a day and very warm. Before I go any further, I must thank both you and Isabel for the parcels of biscuits which you sent and which arrived safely a few days ago. They were just lovely and I can tell you I did enjoy them, especially after trying the biscuits which we can buy here. Since the war began sugar has been very scarce in France and England and consequently the biscuits are not very sweet; and to make matters worse there is a lot of maize meal or some other rubbish put in them, so you can guess they are nothing flash. The only thing flash about them is the price: they cost about a penny each. The biscuits which Isabel made with the jam in them kept beautifully (she asked me to let her know about them) and the others too, and were hardly broken at all; nor were the ones which you sent. I guess they must have had a good trip over and a quick one too.

We are out of the line for three or four days just now and I am going to try and send that matchbox and pendant I told you about, as it is easier to send it from here than in the line. I will try and collect a few more things to send to you all later on when we get out for a rest, which ought to be sometime in the next three years (?) if the Tommies keep on running things the way they have done lately. It is the limit. We have been in the line for nine weeks now instead of eighteen days, while in the villages behind us there are Tommies who have never been in at all yet. The heads are afraid to put them in – they cannot be trusted one minute – and in the face of this the King says NZ & Australia are not doing their bit. However, enough about that. If the censor reads this letter, probably I will get a couple of years in clink, but anyway it is safe there.

I suppose it is winter over there now and pretty cold. It is just the reverse here and the spring is well advanced and it is very warm indeed. Some of the crops, which in some cases are right up in the spaces between the trenches, are just beginning to come to a head. I think the most of the crop about here seems to be barley. We are camped in a very beautiful place now on the summit of a hill and as far as one can see there is nothing but lovely rolling downs, all down in crop, with every here and there a forest of huge trees.[36] They are great on trees in this country and the Froggies plant millions of them in their villages and along the roads. I cannot understand the Froggies at all. All their villages are well laid out and nicely planted with trees etc – in fact, they go to no end of trouble to make their villages beautiful – but they spoil the lot by having them all filthy dirty, with no attempt at sanitation at all.

Near where we are camped there is also a camp of Yanks, and last night I went over and had a yarn to a few of them. They are very much after the style of the colonials and I hope they turn out good scrappers. They are a quiet lot and I did not hear one of them guess or calculate. Perhaps that will come later, when old Fritz starts to drop young iron foundries near them. Their uniform is much like ours and is the same colour, but they wear leggings instead of puttees and a funny little folding cap on field service. In the line they will wear our tin lids, and they use our rifles, bombs etc. Some of them speak very queerly and it is hard to understand them, but they seem good chaps all the same.

Well Lizzie, I will stop now as I cannot keep awake somehow today, so I will say goodbye with love to all in NZ.

I remain, Your Loving Brother,

Ira

P.S. I will write a longer letter next time. Perhaps there will be something to write about then.

Dear Lizzie,

I received two letters from you last night, written on different dates in June. I have mislaid them somewhere just for a minute so I cannot tell you the exact dates, as I was that anxious to get on with reading them that I did not bother much about the dates anyway. I had not received any letters for quite a long while (some I believe had been lost at sea) and I was getting quite downhearted when yours arrived and cheered me up a bit. By the same mail I received a short note from Len Olliver and he was saying that he had to go into camp, so I suppose Willie will have to go too. I wonder what he will do with the shop? A bit rotten for Stella, isn't it, but I guess it will just about be over by the time they arrive in France, as the Americans are just going to make all the difference, I can tell you. They are arriving over here thick and heavy now and are full of fight and just itching to get at old Fritz. They take no prisoners, so old Jerrie had better look out when they arrive over here in millions.

I have just found my letters again. They fell out of my kit bag and got covered up by my overcoat, which just now is acting the part of blanket, overcoat, counterpane and all the rest of it; in fact it is my whole bed complete. In your last letter you asked a few questions, not quite enough but still some, and that will help a bit. I will answer the questions as you have asked them.

How I am as regards health. I was never better in my life; in fact, the open-air life seems to do all of us good, as long as we get plenty to eat and something in the shape of a bed to sleep on that is not absolutely sopping wet. The food, although there is not too much of it, is very good and well cooked, although the cooks are working under bad conditions, cooking over an open fire in the trench with a few sheets of iron overhead to keep the wet out if it rains. Talking about cook-shops, as we call them, this morning about eleven o'clock old Fritz lobbed a shell slap fair into the officers' cook-shop and blew it all to pieces, two tins of meat or fish being all that was left of the whole outfit. As it happened there was nobody in the place at the time – they were down in a tunnel taking shelter – so there was no one hurt. Lucky, wasn't it? The food is much better now than it was in the wintertime, as there was nothing in the way of vegetables to be had then, but now we are getting potatoes, carrots, onions etc in our stew, and they make all the difference to the old bully beef. By the way, the YMCA people sent a buckshee lot of vegetables up to all the boys who were in the line a few days ago, and I can assure you they went very high. (Buckshee is an Egyptian word meaning free or on the never.) The old YM is some good, I can tell you.

The next question was, where are we. Well, we are in the German trenches, but you need not be alarmed as he has been out of them for at least two years. We are in the old German front line of 1914, in reserve to one of our battalions who are now holding the front line, where we have just put in our eight days – and a very rough time we had of it. He shelled us all the time we were in, night & day, with 4.9 inch shells, and in between dropped Minnies and Pineapples on us.[37] Hard man, old Hans and his cobber Fritz. However, we were lucky and only lost a few men, and most of them were wounded. But to get on. As I said before, we are in the old German front line of 1914, in the exact place where the famous Battle of Gommecourt was fought.

Near us is the famous Gommecourt Forest to which the Germans hung on that desperately that many of them were strangled in their tunnels by the French and British soldiers, of which it took 90,000 to shift them, and then I don't know how they did it. They are exceptionally strong & deep trenches, and as the Germans held them for nearly two years you may guess that nothing was left undone to help make them as secure from attack as possible. The forest is on a rise and these trenches are on the outskirts of it, and the sloping ground which lies between them and our old front line, which is about 700 yds away, is just one tangled mass of rusty barbed wire, stakes, both wooden and iron and pointed on top to make them more of a nuisance, and all manner of tangled and twisted angle iron, railway iron etc, which our guns had to blow up before they could shift old Jerrie. Even now that it is smashed up it is an awful nuisance to get through to the road which runs down the hollow, which at one time was no-man's-land, and if you leave the track it is impossible to get through at all.

Then we come to the trenches themselves, which are about twelve feet deep with duckboards in the bottom with a drain underneath them. Steps made of wickerwork lead from the duckboards to the firesteps, from which place the fighting is done. I will give you a rough sketch of the place and then you will see how hard it must have been to shift him.

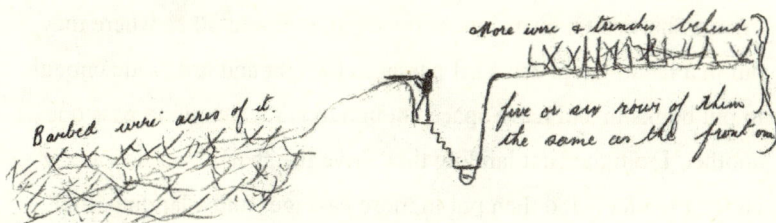

more wire & trenches behind

*five or six rows of them
the same as the front one*

Barbed wire acres of it.

You will see that he would take some shifting even out of one trench, but when you consider that there were about a half a dozen other such trenches behind the front one, with communication trenches connecting them up, you will understand what our chaps were up against. It must have been awful and no mistake. I am glad I was not there, anyway. I suppose you are wondering where old Fritz lived during his long stay in these trenches, so I will tell you. You read a lot in NZ papers about old Fritz sacrificing his men etc etc, but when I tell you <u>we</u> in the front line have very often to make a tiny bivvie, a hole in the bank and our oil sheet for a door, and then I will describe his way of housing his men and leave you to form your own opinion of who had the best time of it. They lived in tunnels, in some cases as deep as eighty feet under the ground, and even the shallowest ones are about thirty feet down and quite safe from even the biggest shell which is likely to be used on the front line. They are lined with wood and fitted with double bunks made of wire netting. I know all about them, you see, as we are living in them at the present time. These tunnels are built right in the front line, and old Fritz must have grinned to himself as he sat away down in them and heard our shells bursting harmlessly overhead; however, it is now our turn to do the grinning.

I will describe the tunnels first and then sketch them, and that will give you a good idea of what they are like. To begin with they drive a shaft down on a slant to the depth of about 30 ft, where they put in a landing and drive off passages to right and left, wide enough to put bunks in and leave space enough to allow people to pass one another. From the first landing they drive the shaft lower down, say another ten feet, and then put in more passages and a landing, then on again and repeat the process as often as needful, according to the number of men which the tunnels are required to hold. Along the trench about two chains they sink another shaft, and when they are down the right depth they put in a landing and passages the same as the first and join their passages with the first lot, making one long passage joining two shafts, which now gives two openings instead of one to the tunnels. They continue on down to the second landing where they do the same, then on to the third where they do likewise. Then they sink more shafts and do the same again until the whole place is one network of underground tunnels with shafts, fitted with gas-proof doors, leading to the surface. They are bon affairs, but old Jerrie has left three things for us which he was welcome to take away with him: namely mice, lice and rats, of which there are millions in these tunnels. I will now try and draw a sketch of the tunnels for you, looking at them from two positions, straight on and sideways. Hope you can make head & tail of the sketch, I cannot.

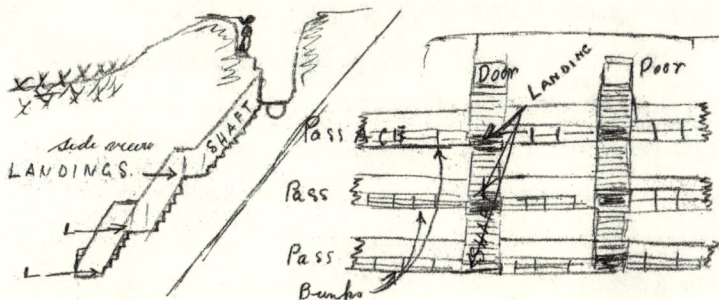

We have just had tea. Perhaps it would give you a good idea of how we live if I told you what we had. We had bacon (fried), cabbage & potatoes and, of course, tea. They were new potatoes and were very good, and I think the YMCA supplied the cabbage but I am not sure. Anyway that was very good too. By the way, if ever you are over-burdened with cash after the war is over you will be able to see this place just as it is today, as the French government is going to leave it just as it is when the war finishes for tourists to come and see. It seems a bit of a tall yarn, but it is a dinkum fact, that our boys are busy on fatigue from here building model trenches to help to make it interesting for them; and mind you old Fritz can shell us easily here, and he does so too at times. Not bad, is it? However, it all goes to show that they are expecting the war to finish soon, and I hope they are right for once. Perhaps it would interest you to know that I am writing this letter in the sentry box at the mouth of one of the tunnels, and everyone seems to take a delight in walking up and down and getting in my light. I guess it is my own fault for getting in such a place, but there is a sort of table and chair in here, which makes all the difference when one is writing a letter.

We always manage to get plenty of clothes, and whenever we get a bath – usually about once a week, unless we are in the line when it is about once in three weeks – we get a change of underclothes & a clean towel, but the most of us carry an extra towel about with us, also a pair or two of socks. We would carry a shirt or two as well only our packs get too heavy, especially if the roads are muddy and wet and you have a Lewis gun doing its best to strangle you or break your neck.

I don't know whether I am supposed to tell you or not, but we have had several American soldiers attached to the NZ division to gain experience in trench warfare; in fact, we have had several thousands of them. They are as a rule quiet, decent sort of chaps, but all the same they are very keen, and the Lord help Fritz when they get going properly. They will settle him up, I guess. They talk quite different from what we do and put things quite a different way. For instance, they would not say C Company, they would say Company C; and they never walk anywhere, they <u>hike</u>; and they all wear shoes, no matter if they are water-tights half way up to their knees; and they always refer to their tea as supper. They wear funny little caps when not in the line, like airmen or something, but of course in the line they wear a steel lid like us; in fact, they are very much the same as us in their dress & equipment. I had one on my Lewis gun team with me in the line last time and his Number was 2,472,763 and J.O. Hanna was his name. He came from Pennsylvania. You can get a good idea of how many there are here by his number, and they are arriving at the rate of 10,000 per day, so I do not see the use of poor little NZ bleeding herself to death for men the way she is doing at present. It is absurd when you think of it, but I suppose it cannot be helped.

I do not want you to neglect poor Bob on my account, and if you have time only to write one letter write to him first, as I guess I get more letters than he does and you can rest assured I will write to you all whether I receive any letters or not, as I know how uncertain the mail service is just now. I have written two letters to him in England, but I have not received an answer from him so far, although he wrote me a short note from Sling Camp. If all goes well I may see Bob when we go out this time, as we are going near the reinforcement camp where the new arrivals usually stay a while. I am going to look him up, anyway, if he is there.

In Len Olliver's letter he sent a cutting out of the newspaper with a description of J. Ware's reception home. They made an awful fuss of him considering he was not in the firing line more than a few hours at the most, and there are thousands of poor chaps over here who have been here for years and are that unlucky that they cannot even get a trip to Blighty with a wound, let alone a trip to NZ. Some chaps are lucky and don't know it. Some more mail came in tonight but there were no letters for me, although I am expecting a few more, so I think I will stop writing for tonight and if I get a few more letters tomorrow I will be able to write a whole lot more. I am going to send in this letter a PC of an American training camp. It was given to me in the front line by the aforesaid American with the almighty number to his name.

I hope you have received the paperknife which I sent to you, as it took quite a lot of sweat and swearing to make that, I can assure you, and besides it was a novelty. Let me know if you receive it or not. Later on I am going to send home a money belt of badges and buttons which I want you to keep for me. The buttons etc are nothing, but to me each has a little history. I am also going to try and send a couple of matchboxes home too. They are made of metal from a bombing Gotha which came down.[38]

Well, here I am still going and I was going to stop quite a long while ago. Anyway I am going to stop now, so good night.

I have just thought of something. I put that letter inside another one I sent to NZ in a green envelope. I will tell you whose letter it was in later on some day. 'There's a hole in the riggin''. Good night.

I left this letter unfinished the other night, thinking I might be able to write a little more today, but I seem to have done my dash somehow, so I will say goodbye with love to all in good old NZ.

I remain, Your Loving Brother,

Jim

Rouen

Dear Lizzie,

Just a few lines to let you know I am still getting along all serene and having rather a good time, although I have been in hospital since I wrote to you last. I was not wounded, but came in because I had a beautiful boil on my neck and was not able to use the L. gun. I was very lucky, as our boys had a bit of a stunt since I left them.[39] The casualty list will speak for itself later on, I suppose. Anyway, I was lucky to be away at the time. I am not going to write very much this time as I will write you a longer letter later on telling you all the news. In the meantime do not worry about me, as I am in a safe place and am doing all right.

I remain, Your Loving Brother,

Ira

France

10 September 1918

Dear Lizzie,

I am going to start a letter to you tonight, but I don't think I will
be able to finish it as I want to go to a picture show which is being
given buckshee in the Salvation Army Hut. Anyway I can start it and
can finish it later on. They say a thing begun is half done; I wonder
if that applies to the war, a glass of beer, or a letter or what?

One of the reasons I am writing to you is because I wrote the
other day a decent long letter to Dulcie, but I am afraid she will not
get it as I made a mistake about the posting of it. I will tell you
about it some other time when I write. I suppose you are wondering,
too, where that letter came from which I wrote and which was
posted in ChCh; about that too I will tell you another time. 'There's
a hole in the riggin'', as Dad used to say.

This is a very decent camp I am in just now, a sort of port of call
on my way back to the battalion. I will tell you all about it except the
name, which I am not allowed to mention in case you should tell old
Fritz. However, to begin with we have a good canteen where one can
buy almost anything, a meal of cooked fresh fish included, which
goes very high I can tell you. The fish are fresh, too, as we are only
a few miles from one of France's most popular watering-places, a
very beautiful place which I will tell you all about some day. All I
can say just now is that it has one of the finest esplanades in the
world from which you can get a fine view of the English Channel,
up and down which steamers seem to pass continually. However, I
am getting right away from camp, and to do that we have to apply

for a pass and then we have to be back in camp at 9.30 sharp.

The canteen is all right, but the two nice girls serving behind the counter draw most of the customers. I will tell you all about it. You see it is like this; some poor chap wants to say a few words to the girls and having no money he has no excuse to do so really, so he waits quietly until he finds out something they may happen to have run out of, then he bustles up as large as life and asks for it with not a cent in his pockets, and when he is told it is off he stands there still asking questions, such as, when will you have it again, what price will it be, large or small tin etc etc, until his mate grabs him and drags him out of the way of other customers waiting to be served. I can tell you this old war has made some schemers one way and another.

I think that just about finishes the canteen. Now we have the YMCA, a bon affair comprising a Hall, Canteen, Billiard Room, Writing and Reading Room, where I am writing now, practically all under the same roof. The Hall is used for pictures & dances, I will tell you about the dances later. The Canteen, Billiard Room and Writing & Reading Rooms need no describing, except that the reading room is both large and comfortable and one can see almost any NZ paper there. The dances are great affairs, 5 francs admission, which pays for a double ticket, and I believe a good supper etc. I suppose you will be wondering where the ladies come from, but when you know we have a WAAC's camp just near us I need say no more, except that there are some very fine girls amongst them. The music for the dances is supplied by the camp orchestra, which by the way is a very good one, as all the good players of any sort of instrument usually stay in this camp or in the camps in England. I must stop now as I want to see that picture show, so goodbye for the present.

I went to the picture show last night and it was very good. I did enjoy it as I had not been to see any pictures for quite a long time. I wish I had kept on writing yesterday now, as I could have written a book then and now I do not feel at all like writing. Funny, isn't it, how you can write some days and not others, but I suppose by the time the poor old censor reads even this much he will be thinking it is quite long enough.

Besides the YMCA and canteen, we have a large hut run by the Salvation Army in which pictures are shown and where one can write letters or have a game of ping-pong or almost any game. The Presbyterians and RCs also have rooms etc, so you see we are well provided for in that respect. There is also in the camp a beautiful 'Bath House', both plunge and shower, built by money given by a NZ lady. She also found the money to help build the YMCA. At one time a good many more troops used to camp here than is the case today and the camp was built to accommodate them, and now when there is not so many it is decent, no rush or scramble for meals and no overcrowding of tents. There is only one thing against this camp and that is you can spend too much money and I am always broke before payday. We can only draw 14/8 and that has to do us 14 days, so you have to go pretty steady. However, if we could get hold of £5 it would be all the same.

During our day's work yesterday I had occasion to go down the road leading out of the camp and in doing so passed a huge cemetery containing thousands of graves, all of which are beautifully kept in order by English girls, Land Girls I think they are called, and I was quite taken with the dress which they wear, and which looks real well. To begin with they wear boots and leggings or else long boots reaching nearly to their knees. Then a pair of khaki breeches, like riding breeches. On top of this is a sort of loose blouse and skirt combined, with a belt at the waist and the skirt reaching nearly to the knees. On their heads they usually wear a felt hat or large peaked cap. They look real well in their rig out, and I guess for the work they are doing are far more comfortable than a long skirt would allow them to be. Girls do a mighty lot of work over here in the back areas I can tell you, and most of the motor cars are driven by them. Also they do a good deal of cooking in the different camps, especially the Tommie camps, where they manage the whole mess halls, waiting on the tables, washing up and everything, and I am told they boss the poor Tommies round wholesale and are far worse even than their officers. I remember seeing a girl in charge of a kitchen once give a poor old Tommy old enough to be her father a terrible talking too, and the poor chap was very near crying, fair dinkum he was, and his knees were knocking together he was that scared. It was a good joke, but not for him, and the Lord help that girl's husband if she ever gets one.

When I was in Rouen I met a rather decent young chap and he was very anxious to hear all about NZ, so I gave him Roland's address and told him to write. If Roland would send him a few PC of different places I would be much obliged, as he did me one or two good turns & if I had been staying in Rouen I am sure he would have seen that I had a good time.

I saw by one of the papers that our Willie had been called up in the ballot. What in the world is he going to do with the shop? Poor

Stella, I guess it will be pretty rotten for her. However, I think it will be pretty nearly over before he gets over here if we can only keep on as we are doing at present, and I do not see why we should not as we are getting stronger every day now and Jerrie is getting weaker.

Well Lizzie, I guess I will have to stop now as I have just about written myself to a standstill, so I will say goodbye with love to all in good old NZ.

I remain, Your Loving Brother,

Ira

P.S. I have not had any letters for week & weeks. I guess I will get a good dose when they do arrive.

WRITE HOME FIRST.

Heatherston   **MILITARY CAMP.**

DATE, _Sunday 28 Jan_ **1916**

First of all it is made of a sort of Grey Green stiff webb[ing]
very coarse canvas. There is to begin with a broad
which goes round the waist and is really the main
the lot, it is about   can be short
or lengthen...
to

are exceptionally strong & deep trenches and as
Germans held them for nearly two years you
...ay guess that nothing was left undone to help
make them as secure from attack as possible.
The forest is on a rise and these trenches are on the
outskirts of it and the sloping grounds which lies
between them and our old Front line which is
about 700 yds away there is just one tangled
mass of rusty barbed wire, stakes both wooden
and iron, and pointed on top to make them
more of a nuisance, and all manner of tangled
...s twisted angle iron rail   on etc which
...o blow up before they could ...st is smashed up it ...to the

that they can tip th[e]
...way when going unde[r]
which are not very
this
(in normal position)
...h two locks on
...we were raise[d]
...e next about 6
...rinciple on
I will not
Joe ought
the beau...

Shakespeare Hut [40]
10 October 1918

Dear Lizzie,

I am just going to write you a few lines to let you know I am now on leave in London and am having a real enjoyable time. I am waiting here for a few days to see if I can find out where Bob is camped and then I am going to try and see him. Afterwards I am going to Scotland, if all goes well and the weather is anything like decent. It is just getting a wee bit on the cold side now. I spent one night at Mr Bob Ellison's place and of course enjoyed myself fine, and last night Frank and I went to a play called 'The Naughty Wife', something quite new.[41] It was a fine play but the dresses which were worn took my eye, they were something beautiful. I never saw anything so fine in the way of dresses before.

I am not going to spend much of my time writing a long letter today, time is too precious over here, but when I get back to France I will write and tell you all about everything and where I have been. So far I have not been out of London.

I will now stop for the present and will write again later on.

I remain, Your Loving Brother,

Ira

Southwark Military Hospital,
London S.E.

Dear Lizzie,

You will be pleased to know that at last I have managed to stop a decent Blighty and am now having a great old time in a cosie bed at the above address, and I can tell you it is the best Front I have ever held. It will do me for the duration. I had only been back from leave two days when I got hit and it was just a little beauty. I will tell you about it.

We were just going to have breakfast and I was walking along with my dixie when a small shell commonly known as a Whizz-Bang lobbed just near us, about fifteen feet away, and wounded a sergeant and myself. I got it in the fleshy part of the thigh at the back of the leg about half way up. Luckily it missed the bone & sinews etc and only cut a piece of flesh clean away, making a decent clean job of it. I was able to walk out to the first dressing station and from there I travelled in motor ambulances to the C.C.S. and from the C.C.S. in an ambulance train to the hospital in France.[42] I am not going to tell you much about it in this part of the letter, later on I will do so.

I had a short letter from Bob just before I left France and then he was doing fine and was keeping in good health. I reckon if he can manage to dodge old Fritz for another month or so the old war will be finished, and a good job too. A funny thing happened to me in France. I landed up in the No 4 General Hospital near Etaples, and after he had gone I discovered that Fred Baldwin had been in the same ward as myself and had left in the middle of the night – while I was asleep – for Blighty with a wound in the arm, which arm I do not know.[43] I believe he joined up with the 2nd Battalion of the NZRB while I was on leave. Two of the Pidgeon boys also joined the battalion and one, if not the two, of them were killed near a small village called Metz near Cambrai.[44] They also joined up while I was on leave.

I was going to tell you all about the journey from the line to the hospital in England. I will describe my own trip as best I can and I guess most trips are much the same. One thing I want you to notice and that is the food which is given to the patients while they are in France. Well, to get on. I was wounded just as it was breaking daylight in the morning and as it was not very severe I bound it up myself. The sergeant, who was wounded in the arm at the same time, and myself reported to the O.C. and then made ourselves as scarce as possible, hobbling away down to our advanced dressing station as quickly as possible. There the old quack had a look at the bandages and as they were all serene he left them alone. Then they took a few particulars – Name, No., unit etc etc – gave us a drink of the best tea I think I have ever tasted and some biscuits, and handed us over to the stretcher-bearers. As we were both walking cases at that time they did not need to carry us, so only one came with us as a guide. The guide took us about three miles to another dressing station, also an NZ one, where the motor ambulances start from for the 3rd Field Ambulance, also an NZ outfit. At this dressing station the boys could not do enough for us and gave us a good meal of cold ham, bread, butter, tea & biscuits, also cigarettes to anyone who smoked. As our bandages were still serene they did not touch them, and after a little while the motors arrived and away we went to the NZ 3rd Field Ambulance. There we received every attention, got a drink of cocoa and some more biscuits. Here also our wounds were dressed and we were inoculated against lockjaw or something or other; then we were put on more motors and taken away down to Cambrai to a big Tommie C.C.S. composed of hundreds of big tents. When we left our own Field Ambulance we also left any decent treatment that we were likely to get. I would like to say right here that the Canadian, Australian, Scottish or any C.C.S. bar those lousy British ones are very good indeed, but the most of the British ones & also their hospitals in France are a disgrace to the British Army. I am like the Yanks, I can't stick those damn British nohow. All they can do is talk, and then they misplace their Hs.

However, to get on. Where was I? I forgot to mention that at the 3rd Field Ambulance we got our clearance card, which consists of a waterproof envelope with a card inside, which is tied on to your coat button as long as you have a coat and after that it is pinned on to your pyjamas as long as you are on the move, and when you arrive at the hospital it is hung at the head of your bed with your temperature chart and religion disc. On the card is written your name, age, unit, number, religion etc, and as you pass through the different dressing stations or hospitals it is stamped with their stamp, and if they treat your wound in any way it is also written on the back of the card by the doctor who treats you and also the time that he did so.

After a good long ride in the motors we arrived at the Tommie C.C.S. near Cambrai where we were welcomed by a meal of tinned stew, warmed up and dumped on the tables tins and all, dry bread & tea. When you consider that two thirds of the men were hit in the arms and hands, and the rest of us in the legs, feet and hips, I don't think it would have hurt them to put the stew on plates for the boys with only one arm. Instead the chaps with good arms and bad legs had to look after the rest as best they could. We should have only stopped there for a few hours, but owing to an accident to the train we were there 24 hours and it was awful. It was a very cold day and the only place we had to go was in a big tent where dozens of stretchers were laid in rows on the floor, or I should say ground, there was no floor. For tea we had bread and jam and tea and had to wait about an hour in a queue before we got it then. After tea we were given a blanket each and told to make ourselves as comfortable as possible for the night. And an awful night we had. There were about a hundred of us in the tent and all of us were freezing with the cold and the groans of those who were severely hit were terrible to hear all night long. I was glad when morning came and we lined up again for breakfast, which consisted of bread, jam & tea. After breakfast we were loaded up in ambulances and driven about 20 miles to another hospital near a place called Ypres. Here we were given a drink of tea and some biscuits, at least the others were; I was given a dose of clohoroform (that's not spelt right but it does not matter) and the cut in my leg was sewn up and dressed and my clothes taken away. From there on I was a stretcher case, dressed up like a sore finger in pyjamas, and my ticket tied on to me like a sack of coal.

When I woke up after the operation the first thing I heard was a terrible jabbering and I thought to myself I must be in China. Then I had a drink of tea and some biscuits and then some more sleep. Later I discovered the cause of all the jabbering I had heard when I first awoke. From this hospital to the ambulance trains the patients who could not walk were conveyed on light trolleys carrying four at a time, and these trolleys were loaded and unloaded by Chinks and the sinners jabber continually.[45] The night I went out the Chows managed to upset one of the trolleys and spill four men down the bank and that was the cause of all the talking. However, I was not upset and landed safely in the bunk on the train. In our train there were several wounded German prisoners sitting, and when the Chinks saw them they grinned like monkeys, showing about a yard of yellow teeth, and said, pointing at them with a grimy finger, 'Jellie plisoner, no bon ha,' a queer mixture of French, Chow and Tommie slang.

When we were all loaded the train set off and as I slept a good part of the way, being night-time, I cannot tell you much about it except that they woke me up and gave me a piece of bread and cheese & cup of tea, which was all we had for tea. In the morning (we were on the train all night) we had some bully beef and bread and tea for breakfast. About 10am in the morning we arrived at our destination, a hospital near Etaples, and there we were unloaded into motors again and taken to a Tommy hospital, the 4th General. Being in bed I had nothing to do but sleep and eat, that is when I could get anything to eat. Luckily, on each side of me were two boys who had been gassed and could not eat much, so I used to come to the rescue and eat their dinner as well as my own and even then I was still hungry, it was rotten. I was glad to get away. I stayed there about five days and I will tell you what they used to give us for our meals each day. For breakfast we had stiff porridge, without any milk or sugar, one slice of bread and butter & tea, very weak and cold without any sugar. If we had no porridge we had L/Cpl Bacon (one stripe) instead, which was worse. For dinner we had one piece of

(<u>tough</u>) beef, a spoonful of watery gravy and a potato boiled in its jacket, followed by a pudding of sorts, usually ground rice, drowned with water without a single grain of sugar or flavouring of any sort. It was for all the world like paste, only not so tasty I bet. You bet I did enjoy it. For tea we had $1\frac{1}{2}$ slices of bread & butter & tea, and for supper a little thin soup and a piece of bread. You will think I am a terrible growler, but fair dinkum, the food was rottenly cooked and everything. I was disgusted with the whole outfit. I was there five days and then I came across in the hospital ship, and about that trip I will tell you later as I am sick of writing today. My neck is all kinked with sitting up so long writing.

Just before I got wounded I received three parcels from Dulcie and I must thank her very much for sending them. Also I got about a dozen letters, several of yours among them, and I thank you very much all of you for writing, and you also for the YMCA coupons which I can use even although I am in England. Among the parcels I got was one of lollies and on the afternoon I got it old Fritz attacked, but I was determined he would not get any of my lollies so I popped the last half dozen in my mouth all at once, paper and all, and carried on although nearly choked by them until we stopped the attack, which only lasted half an hour.

I will now close my letter with love to you all, and I hope it will not be necessary to send any more boys from NZ as I think the end is very near now.

I remain, Your loving Brother,

Ira

P.S. I was pleased you got the paperknife all right.

Dear Lizzie,

I am only going to write you a short note today as I don't feel a bit like writing and I think when one does not feel like writing they always write a very poor sort of a letter.

The last time I wrote to you I was in the Southwark Military Hospital, London, but since then I have been shifted to the New Zealand Convalescent Hospital, Hornchurch and it is very much better here in every way. To begin with there are only NZ boys here and of course we get on all right together and that is the main thing. Then the food is ever so much better and there is plenty of it, and I have always found no matter where you are if the food is good the place is all right to be in as the boys are always more contented and happy. I guess there is a good deal of the pig in the NZ soldier. Keep him full and give him plenty of blankets and he is happy and will not give much trouble, but half starve him and limit him to one blanket and he will give no end of trouble. Perhaps that is why the Australians call us Pig Islanders.

Since I came to England I have received several parcels from NZ, two from Dulcie and one from Ada, and I thank everyone for sending them. Nearly all the boys are going back to NZ from Hornchurch so if I have any luck at all I may land NZ too later on, but it will not be for a month or two as there is a terrible lot of chaps to go first.

This is some camp, I can tell you. We have a huge YMCA and a War Contingent Association Hut and there are all manner of different places where one can go and spend the evenings, pictures, concerts etc. I am going to get some views of the place and later on when I get settled down I will write and tell you all about it. I have not had time to see it all yet myself.

I will close my letter now, hoping you are all well in good old NZ.

I remain, Your Loving Brother,

Ira

Hornchurch Convalescent Hospital,
England
2 DECEMBER 1918

Dear Lizzie,

As you see I have been shifted since I wrote to you last and I am
now in Hornchurch Con Camp, and I can assure you it is much
better than being in the Tommie hospital in London.

Well, I don't know I am sure what I am going to write about this
morning, although it is up to me to write a decent long letter as I
received a dozen letters yesterday and nearly a dozen while I was in
the Southwark Hospital.

The hospital is about 30 miles from London and I should say
there are roughly about 2,000 chaps in it, or I should say what is left
of them, as some have an arm off, some a leg, some an eye out and
so on, until you begin to wonder if there are any whole men left in
the NZ division. I can tell you it makes you realise how lucky you
are to get out of it all with only a slight wound. The patients live in
huts holding about 30 men each, and in marquees which are smaller
and only hold about 15 or twenty men. The huts have coal heaters in
them and the marquees have gas heaters. It is very cold of a night
now and I can tell you we keep the old heaters going all night long. I
am in a marquee and it is all right as we only have to light the gas
and away she goes without any trouble about stoking etc, like the
coal heaters.

We are allowed plenty of leave here; we are allowed anywhere
within five miles of the camp any day between the hours of 3pm and
9pm, and on Saturday from 12 noon until 9pm. Also two out of each

tent or hut can, by applying to the orderly room, get a pass to London starting from 9am and expiring at 9pm, on Saturday or Sunday. The leave is all right, but as we have only our hospital pay to do it on we have to be careful or else we run out of cash quick and lively. We get 7/6 a week here, but in the Tommie hospitals they only pay you 10/- every four weeks and that is no use at all in London these days when everything is so dear. Talk about things being dear, a lady visiting the hospital in London told me that she went in to buy a hare and they wanted 12/- for it, and then she priced a rabbit and they wanted 7/6 for that, so she gave it up as a bad job. Isn't that an awful price, and I guess in NZ people will hardly buy rabbits & hares at any price at all.

Well, to get on about Hornchurch. As far as I can make out the camp is in part of some gentleman's estate lent to the NZ military people, or perhaps rented. They also have the use of the residence, which has been converted into a hospital for the serious cases. It is called Grey Towers; I will send you some views of it later on. In the camp, which is divided from Grey Towers by an iron fence, we have a huge YMCA building, in the writing room of which I am writing this letter. I will tell you about it, it is some place. First of all there is a big concert hall which will easily hold 900 or a thousand men, and every night there is something on, either pictures or a concert, or a lecture or something. Next to that there is a huge room filled with small tables and chairs and lounges, with three or four fireplaces to keep it nice and warm. At one end of this room there is a counter where you can buy at certain hours a cup of tea, coffee or cocoa or malted milk and a cake, biscuit or scone. You are only allowed to buy one scone at a time, you know, as the food is none too plentiful over here even now the war is over; in fact, in the camp mess rooms is about the only place where you can get a decent meal. I suppose it will gradually work back to pre war conditions, but it will take some time.

As you know, all NZ soldiers when they are convalescent and on the way home on the boat are compelled to attend a certain number of educational classes, and the YMCA people have built several beautiful classrooms in this building to hold the different classes in. For instance, there is one room for stained glass and drawing, another for motor engineering and electricity, another for book-keeping and shorthand, another for arithmetic, another for wood-working and wood-carving, and another for wool classing and agriculture. Besides these there is a big billiard room, a bank and a stationer's stall and a kitchen all under the one roof, so you see it is quite a big affair, isn't it? I have not decided what class I will take on yet. I think I am a bit lazy. I don't seem to want to be bothered with any of them somehow, but I suppose I will have to learn something. Besides the YMCA we have a place run by the War Contingents Association, which is practically the same as the YM except that there are no classrooms in connection with it. Then we have a wet and dry canteen, which is run by the military people and is no good at all. Then there is the usual array of orderly rooms, wash houses, bath houses and clink, and other camp fixtures which altogether make quite a little township.

The cooking in this camp is done by girls and the food is dished out in the mess room by girls too, and they make a better job of it than the men usually do. I suppose you wonder how they manage to feed all the men without getting all in a muddle, so I will tell you.

The men in the camp are divided up into different Companies and each Company has its own mess room. The mess rooms will seat about 200 men at a sitting. All the men have to line up outside the mess room door and come in in single file down the centre. Half way down the room are four girls dishing out the food and as you pass the table where they are you pick up a plate of food, and if it is dinner time you take a plate of pudding and a plate of meat and vegetables or whatever it is. You then continue on down the room and take your place at one of the tables, filling up the tables from one end of the room as you go. The bread, and butter & cheese or jam, if there is any, is put on the table and you help yourself to it. When you have finished you take your knife & fork and spoon and wash them in a bucket of boiling water just outside the mess room door and take them away with you, and you keep them all the while you are in camp. It is a very good way of doing it I can tell you, and the whole lot of us are fed and out of the place inside of half an hour.

Oh, about our beds etc in the marquees. We each have an iron bedstead with spring mattress with a flax mattress on top of it, two sheets, two pillows and pillow slips, which are changed each week, and five blankets, so you see they intend us to sleep warm anyway, don't they?

I did not finish your letter the other day so I will try and finish it today, but I am not going to write very much or else I will not be able to find anything to write about next week when I write.

While I think of it, I saw Fred Baldwin last night at the pictures and he reckons he will soon be away back to NZ once again. I guess he was lucky, don't you? He said the smack he got was not very severe and that it will not trouble him at all in after life. I can manage to get about all right now and I am going to have a look round the country a bit later on, and then I will have something to write about as I have just about written the camp to death.

I think I will stop just now and I will write some more some other time when I feel like writing.

I remain, Your Loving Brother,

Ira

New Zealand Convalescent Hospital,
Hornchurch, Essex, England
15 DECEMBER 1918

Dear Lizzie,

I received your letter written 16 Oct on Saturday, that is a couple of days ago, all by itself. Goodness only knows how it came wandering along all on its own. I was reckoning on getting some more today but so far I have not got any; however, there is another mail today yet so my luck may be in after all. Anyway, I will not finish up your letter in case some more letters do arrive from NZ and I find something more to write about.

Of course, you know by now Bob came through the scrapping over in France all right. He missed the last stunt as he was a bit off colour, and when he wrote to me the other day he said he was going before a medical board, and if he does not land an NZ out of it I don't know what I am talking about. They are bundling the NZ boys home as quickly as possible and yours truly may be on the water by the time you receive this letter. I hope so anyway, as I don't care how soon I leave this side of the world, which is cold and wet and miserable and all upside down.

I saw Fred Baldwin here one night at the pictures, but as he went away out on leave a day or so after I have not seen any more of him. He told me he was in France seven days and saw quite enough of it to satisfy him for life. He was lucky enough to get just a nice little smack, just enough to send him to Blighty. I guess by now you will want a map of Germany if you are going to keep the front line in sight. It is an awful pity we could not get a smack at a few more of

132

those Fritzes now they are beat. No mistake, the sinners knew when to give in just as well as they knew when to make a stunt. If it had not been for those Yanks coming in when they did, goodness only knows when the war would have finished. I don't. Never mind, it is over now and Bob and I are both safe and well and Roly and Willie will not have to go into camp, so we have a mighty lot to be thankful for.

I knew Ada & Willie were thinking of going to the N.I. but I had no idea they were going to make such a clean sweep of their live & dead stock, furniture etc etc. I say, what will Willie do without the ferrets etc, to say nothing of the flute? Did poor old Wag manage to escape or did he die or what happened to him? Anyway, I hope they get on all right where-ever they go and that the weather conditions will suit them better up north. I have met several boys from Hamilton and they all say without exception that it is a place that is going ahead wonderfully. I hope it is so.

I don't half like the idea of going back to carpentering when I return to NZ so I guess I will have to go in for duck or something as you suggest, if there is plenty of money to be made out of them, as money now the war is over seems the only thing that is likely to worry one.

I was sorry to hear that the children had been bad with the flu. There are thousands & thousands of people ill in England and Europe with the same wretched thing.[46] They do not seem to be able to stamp it out here at all, and now the sinners are inoculating all the soldiers against it. Every soldier is inoculated in the arm twice against it, although civilians are allowed to wander all over the country with it taking no precautions at all. Do you know influenza is so bad in some towns in England, Nottingham is one, that soldiers going on leave are not allowed to visit it at all. It is absolutely out of bounds to them.

I was awfully glad to hear my money belt arrived safely in NZ as I was wondering whether it had gone to the bottom or not. I think a mighty lot of that belt I can tell you, each button on it means something to me. I did not like parting with it even to send it back to NZ as I used to say it brought me good luck, and I would as soon go in the line without my gas mask as that belt. For instance, the Australian badge at the end, the first one I put on the belt, came from Passchendaele, where I got it on 13 Oct 1917, the day after we made that rotten stunt there. I remember it well. There was a terrible explosion and when the mud had finished falling we found two men dead and their equipment blown off them and their kit bags, or I should say their valise, a small bag carried when going over the top, blown to pieces. Some of their gear landed near me, and on looking at it I found it was the aforesaid Australian badge and a Froggie knife. The Froggie knife I still have and I hope to fetch it home with me.

It is so long since I sent the parcel away that I almost forget what was in it now, but I think I remember putting a little pendant made out of aluminium in it. The aluminium came off a German bombing plane which came down and was captured by the N. Zealanders near a big Chateau called Chateau De La Hare, or something like that.[47] By the way, we never got the credit for salving that plane. The blooming Tommies pinched it and carted it away in a motor lorry, our chaps thinking they would be credited with it, but they never were. Those Tommies are rotters and no mistake.

I will have to leave off now as it is mail time and I have to go and fetch it for our tent, being in charge of it, so goodbye for the present.

The reason why there were English stamps on that parcel was because I got a chum of mine who was over on leave to post it for me, and the little brown cloth bags you mention at one time were part of a small arms ammunition bandolier and contained two clips of rifle cartridges before I cut them off and used them for packing.

I will have to stop now as I want to catch this evening mail, so goodbye with love to all.

I remain, Your Loving Brother,

Ira

Y·M·C·A

THE NEW ZEALAND EXPEDITIONARY FORCES

WRITE HOME FIRST.

Y.M.C.A   Y.M.C.A

Featherston   MILITARY CAMP.

DATE, Sunday 28 Jan 1916

First of all it is made of a sort of Grey Green stiff webb~~
~~ry coarse canvas. There is to begin with a broad
~~which~~ goes round the waist and is really the main
~~the lot~~, it is about ~~... can~~ be shorte~~
~~ lengthen~~

On Active Service

WITH THE BRITISH EXPEDITIONARY FORCE

are exceptionally strong & deep trenches and as
Germans held them for nearly two years you
~~may~~ guess that nothing was left undone to help
~~make~~ them as secure from attack as possible.
The forest is on a rise and these trenches are on the
outskirts of it and the sloping grounds which lies
between them and our old Front line which is
about 700 yds away there is just one tangled
mass of rusty barbed wire, stakes both wooden
and iron, and pointed on top to make them
more of a nuisance, and all manner of tangled
~~... twisted~~ angle iron ~~rai~~ ~~ron~~ etc which
~~... to blow up before they could~~ ~~... it is smashed up it~~

that they can tip the
way when going under
which are not very ~~...~~
~~thus~~
(in normal position)

~~... h~~ two locks on ~~...~~
~~... we were raised~~
~~... next about 6~~
~~trenciple on wh~~
I will not ~~...~~
Joe ought ~~...~~
the beauty ~~...~~

Despite the doubts expressed in his last letter, Ira did go back to carpentry after the war, setting up in partnership with another man.

In August 1921 he married Sarah Isabella (Bella) Gibson, who came from Coldingham in Scotland and had boarded with the Robinson family. Their children were Enid (b. 1922), David (b. 1923) and Shirley (b. 1925).

During the 1920s Ira worked for the Education Department, and with another man was employed by them to build schools in the Chatham Islands. This took several years, since supplies came in by boat at irregular intervals, and he was able to get back to see his family only occasionally. He returned to self-employment but was hard-hit by the Depression, when the family were very poor. Later he worked at the Lichfield shirt factory in Christchurch.

Ira retired at sixty, but found inactivity boring. He taught carpentry at the Rehabilitation Training Centre in Christchurch for three or four years, and also undertook window dressing jobs at Ballantynes. He died in Christchurch on 11 April 1959 at the age of seventy.

The relationship with his oldest sister remained close, and his daughter Enid recalled as a small child regularly being taken on a bicycle to have tea with 'Auntie Lizzie'.

There is no doubt that Ira was emotionally scarred by his war service. Enid remembered that he was irritated by loud noises, and their mother would often tell the children to keep quiet so as not to upset him. He didn't speak to them of his war experiences, but anyone who reads his letters will hardly find this surprising.

Appendix
THE ROBINSON FAMILY

John Robinson, a sail-maker, was born in Belfast, Northern Ireland in 1808. He married Elizabeth, who was born in Co. Monaghan in 1810 and whose maiden name was also Robinson, although they were unrelated. They had seven children. The oldest, also John, had been ill and was prescribed a long sea voyage for convalescence. He travelled to New Zealand accompanied by his sister Rachel. John was an amateur photographer and earned a good living as a professional working in Dunedin and Central Otago during the gold rush days.

John refused to return to Ireland when he was well again. Rachel went back on her own, but she missed her brother and New Zealand and persuaded her whole family to emigrate. Her father's brother (who may have been named William) and his family also emigrated at the same time.

John senior and Elizabeth left Britain on board the *Mermaid* on 30 September 1865 and arrived in Lyttelton on 1 January 1866. Travelling with them on the voyage were their children Rachel (aged 24), Catherine (22), William (20), Rebecca (16), Isaac (11) and James (10). John died at Lyttelton on 2 September 1876, while Elizabeth lived until 27 September 1894.

John junior, who had remained in New Zealand, married Ellen Selina Moore, the daughter of William and Elizabeth Moore of Okains Bay. In about 1878 John built the Okains Bay Store, then he moved to Pigeon Bay after installing his younger brother William as store manager. A post office extension was added in about 1892, when William became postmaster.

William's son, also William, later succeeded as storekeeper and postmaster and ran the business until 1938, when heavy debts forced him to sell it. The store had its ups and downs in the following years, but is once again flourishing after being purchased by local historian Murray Thacker in 1970.

John senior's daughter Rachel married Robert Best Ellison. He was the son of a Captain Ellison, who was the master of various immigrant ships in the 1860s, and it is possible Rachel met her future husband on one of her voyages. Captain Ellison apparently brought out some capital and set up his son and Rachel on a farm at Otaio, south of Timaru. Most of their ten children were born there, the exception being their second child Elizabeth Best (1868–1941), the only member of the family to achieve public prominence. She married Thomas Edward Taylor, who became a Member of Parliament and Mayor of Christchurch. Elizabeth was closely involved with her husband's political and civic activities and after his death entered public life on her own account, receiving the OBE in 1937.

Rachel's oldest child Robinson (Rob or Bob) Ellison moved to Britain in an official capacity representing New Zealand agriculture. Another of Rachel's children, William John (b. 1878) married his cousin Priscilla Ada Robinson, Ira's sister. The Mr Ellison whom Ira mentions visiting in London was thus Ada's brother-in-law, as well as their cousin, but the formality of Ira's address indicates a considerable age difference between them.

The unusual name of Cardigan Petterson, who married Ira's sister Isabel, deserves an explanation. His parents, Julianna Gustafoa and Jonas Petter Petterson, emigrated from Sweden to New Zealand in 1873 on the British ship *Cardigan Castle*. Julianna was pregnant when they sailed and her child was born on the ship off the coast of Africa on 28 August. The boy was named after the ship and given British nationality.

Jonas Petterson, the son of a nobleman, had been banished by his family for marrying a peasant's daughter. He worked as a blacksmith at Duvauchelle before moving to Le Bons Bay and setting up a smithy there in the late 1870s. Cardigan took over the smithy after Jonas retired, shifting it to Akaroa in 1918. The blacksmith's anvil in the Okains Bay Museum is the one brought out from Sweden by Jonas, and used by him and Cardigan for many years.

Endnotes

1   New Zealand units had a huge variety of badge designs, which made the badges very collectable. In contrast, Australian troops used a universal badge.
2   22nd RFB was a non-standard abbreviation for 22nd New Zealand Reinforcements, New Zealand Rifle Brigade. Troops were sent out regularly from New Zealand as numbered 'reinforcement' units, which were drafted into existing corps at the front.
3   O.C. was the abbreviation for Officer in Command.
4   No information is available on the Ollivers, but it would appear the Robinsons were well acquainted with the family.
5   Rfts was the abbreviation for reinforcements.
6   Sling Camp, situated on the Salisbury Plain 74 miles south-west of London, had been used for manoeuvres by the British Army before it was allocated to the New Zealand Division. The New Zealanders put their stamp on the site by carving a giant kiwi in the chalk hillside overlooking the camp.
7   Zep or, more usually, Zepp, was an abbreviation for Zeppelin.
8   RF was an abbreviation for Royal Field Artillery.
9   K of K is a reference to Kitchener's full title, 1st Earl Kitchener of Khartoum.
10 Jack Ware was born in Okains Bay, where his grandparents had settled in 1852. The Mason boys' grandparents settled in Okains Bay in 1850. Both brothers returned there to farm, though Mick lost a leg in the war.
11 Prince Arthur, Duke of Connaught, was the third son of Queen Victoria.
12 Robinson Ellison was the brother of Ada's husband, William Ellison (see page 139).
13 Nancy, Harry and Lester (properly Leicester) were three of Lizzie's five children. At the date of this letter Harry was seven years old, Leicester five years, and Nancy thirteen months.
14 Blighty was slang for Britain, and smack was a colloquial term for a wound. A 'Blighty smack' was a wound sufficiently disabling to necessitate evacuation to Britain.
15 Tess (Leicester) Ware was Jack Ware's younger brother. He was killed in Christchurch when his car ran into Sunnyside Bridge. The Mould family farmed at German Bay and then Lavericks Bay (where their nine children were born), before moving to Robinsons Bay in 1904. It was probably Harry Mould whom Ira met.
16 The town in question is probably Cassel.
17 This attack was part of the 3rd Battle of Ypres, which began on 31 July 1917 and ended with the capture of the village of Passchendaele on 6 November.
18 'Mr Vaun' may have been Major Vaughan.
19 The French word 'bon', meaning 'good', was adopted as slang by the British and Colonial forces.
20 HE was an abbreviation for high-explosive.

21 Harry Harris, who was part-Maori, farmed at Okains Bay. As well as his one son, Herbert, he had three daughters.

22 The region Ira refers to is around Quesques and Verval.

23 The growing of cocksfoot grass for seed was one of Banks Peninsula's major industries between 1880 and the 1930s. The Robinsons had seed-cleaning machinery in a shed next to the Okains Bay General Store. Ira must have helped with harvesting the tough-headed seed, which had to be flailed by hand.

24 Bella may be Sarah Isabella Gibson, Ira's future wife.

25 The Mackenzies owned the Taitapu pub until the 1960s.

26 The final page of this letter is missing.

27 The Young Men's Christian Association (YMCA) established canteens in the rear areas of the Front.

28 'Bivvie' was an abbreviation for bivouac, and referred to any temporary shelter or dug-out.

29 A dixie was either a camp-kettle or a mess tin.

30 Jack Ware was not killed, but was badly wounded in the elbow. He convalesced in an English hospital and married his nurse; later they settled in New Zealand.

31 Ira John Petterson (b. 20 July 1910) was the son of Ira Robinson's sister Isabel, who married Cardigan Petterson.

32 Sir Douglas Haig was the Commander-in-Chief of the British Expeditionary Force in France.

33 The training area of the New Zealand Division was situated south-west of St Omer, in country that had been one of the training grounds of the French Army. Musketry was practised on the ranges at Moulle, to the north-west.

34 The sector Ira refers to was between Hébuterne and Sailly-au-Bois.

35 The casualties at Brigade headquarters on 28 April were two officers killed and three wounded, and nine men killed and eleven wounded.

36 The area Ira refers to is south-west of Authie.

37 'Minnies' and 'Pineapples' were slang terms for types of mortar bomb.

38 Gotha was a generic term for any large German bomber.

39 The 'stunt' was the 2nd Battle of Bapaume, which began on 21 August.

40 Shakespeare Hut in Russell Square, run by the YMCA, provided accommodation for soldiers on leave.

41 Frank Robinson Ellison was the third son of Robinson (Bob) Ellison and his wife May (née Ballinger), who had eight children in all.

42 C.C.S. was an abbreviation for Casualty Clearing Station.

43 Fred Baldwin was most likely a relative of Lizzie's husband, Joe Baldwin.

44 Both Pidgeon boys, Hector and Henry, were killed. Their brother Vic was married to Harry Harris' sister Lucy.

45 In 1918 almost 100,000 Chinese were serving as labourers with the British on the Western Front.

46 The Spanish flu epidemic began in June 1918 and lasted for about a year. It spread rapidly through a world population weakened by war, killing at least 27 million people.

47 This was Chateau de la Haie, directly west of Gommecourt.